WILLIAM PITT, EARL OF CHATHAM 1708–1778
A Bibliography

Recent Titles in
Bibliographies of British Statesmen

William Pitt the Younger 1759–1806: A Bibliography
A. D. Harvey

Lord Grenville 1759–1834: A Bibliography
A. D. Harvey

Lord Curzon 1839–1925: A Bibliography
James G. Parker

Lord Nelson 1758–1805: A Bibliography
Leonard W. Cowie

The Duke of Wellington 1769–1852: A Bibliography
Michael Partridge

Charles James Fox 1749–1806: A Bibliography
David Schweitzer

George Grenville 1712–1770: A Bibliography
Rory T. Cornish

William Wilberforce 1759–1833: A Bibliography
Leonard W. Cowie

Margaret Thatcher: A Bibliography
Faysal Mikdadi

WILLIAM PITT, EARL OF CHATHAM 1708–1778

A Bibliography

Karl W. Schweizer

BIBLIOGRAPHIES OF
BRITISH STATESMEN, NO. 14

GREGORY PALMER, SERIES EDITOR

Greenwood Press
Westport, Connecticut • London

Library of Congress Cataloging-in-Publication Data

Schweizer, Karl W.
    William Pitt, Earl of Chatham, 1708–1778 : a bibliography / Karl
W. Schweizer.
       p.   cm.—(Bibliographies of British statesmen, ISSN
1056–5523 ; no. 14)
    ISBN 0–313–28293–5 (alk. paper)
    1. Pitt, William, Earl of Chatham, 1708–1778—Bibliography.
2. Great Britain—Politics and government—18th century—
Bibliography. I. Title. II. Series.
Z8694.49.S38   1993
[DA483.P6]
016.94107′3′092—dc20   93–13010

British Library Cataloguing in Publication Data is available.

Library of Congress Catalog Card Number: 93–13010
ISBN: 0–313–28293–5
ISSN: 1056–5523

First published in 1993

Greenwood Press, 88 Post Road West, Westport, CT 06881
An imprint of Greenwood Publishing Group, Inc.

Printed in the United States of America

∞™

The paper used in this book complies with the
Permanent Paper Standard issued by the National
Information Standards Organization (Z39.48–1984).

10 9 8 7 6 5 4 3 2 1

No man was ever better fitted to be the minister in a great and powerful nation, or better qualified to carry that power and greatness to their utmost limits. There was in all his designs a magnitude and even a vastness which was not easily comprehended by every mind and which nothing but success could have made to appear reasonable.

—Edmund Burke, 1761

Contents

Preface

The purpose of the present bibliography is to bring together for the first time a full range of sources relating to the life and career of William Pitt, first Earl of Chatham—perhaps the most complex and fascinating personality on the 18th. century British political stage. Intended as a guide for further research, this volume, accordingly, has attempted to be as comprehensive as possible in its listing of manuscript, printed primary sources and biographical studies relating to Pitt. The sections listing, and annotating, writings about Pitt and his career concentrate largely on works that make important contributions to our understanding of his personal role in issues and events. Some additional titles have also been included when they provide vital background to some aspects of his career. Principal newspapers, journals and magazines of the period and their position on Pitt have been noted; readers must consult relevant indexes for specific items. Since the pamphlet literature on Pitt is absolutely immense, requiring separate bibliographical treatment if every contemporary pamphlet mentioning Pitt were to be listed, only those pamphlets are included in which Pitt is the central focus of discussion or those discussing issues with which Pitt was directly concerned.

The nature of this work and ever escalating cost of domestic and foreign research entails a lengthy list of acknowledgments. I would first like to thank the many record offices, archives and libraries, too numerous to mention individually, who greatly eased my task by their prompt and courteous response to requests for information and assistance. I am especially grateful to the Interlibrary Loan staff at the New Jersey Institute of

Technology for their ever willing help and cooperation. I also wish to acknowledge the generosity of the National Endowment for the Humanities in providing a timely travel grant and the New Jersey Institute of Technology for defraying additional travel costs. Special thanks are also due to Gregory Palmer, editor of this series, for his encouragement and helpful critical suggestions and to Mrs. Cynthia Harris, executive editor of Greenwood Press, for her assistance at different stages in the preparation of this work.

Finally, my wife typed drafts and a final version with a forbearance only those who know my handwriting can appreciate; without her devotion and support this book would not have been completed.

Introduction

Few British statesmen have been as complex, controversial and ambiguous—an enigma to contemporaries and historians alike—as William Pitt the elder, first Earl of Chatham. Acclaimed in his own lifetime and subsequently as a great war leader—the architect of Empire—a man of dynamic energy and vision, Pitt was also recognized for his human failings, possessing a personality which alternately fascinated and repelled: irritable, egotistical, imperious, even arrogant—driven by a restless ambition that inspired resentment, admiration but only rarely affection among the political figures of his day. The problems he encountered in obtaining his first post in the 1740's and high office a decade later are attributable in large measure to the difficulty his temperment and views presented to other politicians and to George II, the king. Pitt's loss of office in 1761, the subsequent failure of his opposition to the Peace of Paris, his disunited and unsuccessful administration (1766–1768) and even his limited impact both in opposition politics (1769–1771) and following the outbreak of the war in America, can all be related to his personal flaws: an inability to cooperate with others for long, to court and conciliate potential supporters and a failure to appreciate differing convictions and points of view. In the words of Frank O'Gorman: "He lacked the capacity for understanding the feelings of others and the fact that their opinions, however much he might disagree with them, were held just as sincerely as his own. In these personal defects lie some of the reasons, at least, why Pitt's career after 1761 was

LORD CHATHAM

one of continuous failure and constant frustration."[1] And yet, his public image—so carefully cultivated—never dimmed, not amidst political setbacks, physical illness or the mental afflictions of his later years; outside the restricted world of Whitehall and Westminster, Pitt remained a heroic figure—the embodiment of patriotism, the nemesis of ministerial ineptitude and vice. "He was seen as the 'Patriot minister', above the dirty work of politics, pursuing the best interests of his country, regardless of personal gain."[2]

This adulatory view of Pitt has been questioned in recent years[3] as has his responsibility for the strategy behind Britain's global victories during the Seven Years War. Thus, revisionist scholarship over the past two decades has suggested that Pitt's contributions to Britain's success have been exaggerated: that the nature of eighteenth century government alone—departmental with ministers responsible only to the King— effectively curtailed the executive authority wielded by any one individual, however politically prominent.[4] By directing attention from Parliament to the Court, from leading ministers and politicians to the Crown, these writings have fostered a reassessment of the British state in which the significance of notable individual figures such as Pitt is necessarily lessened. Visible also in the area of military history, this break with the excessively biographical tendency of older scholarship has correspondingly led to a greater concentration on the bureaucratic, logistical and financial dimensions of Britain's war for empire[5]—on the interplay between strategy and politics and on the modalities of military and naval operations. It now seems unlikely that Pitt, at least at the outset, actually had a comprehensive strategic vision in the sense of a master plan for pursuing the war. If anything, as Middleton has demonstrated,[6] Pitt's celebrated strategy—that of "conquering America in Germany"— was an aggregate of successful experience in previous Anglo-French wars and improvisation, the empirical response to shifting conditions and needs, acquiring distinctive shape and momentum as the conflict evolved. Only in time does Pitt appear to have developed an integrated view of the conflict with France, one which ultimately placed Britain's key objectives, overseas and continental, into an effective balance.[7] At the same time, for all his studied eccentricities, Pitt was a man of unusual gifts: driving energy, animated by the prospect and opportunities of war, singlemindedness of purpose, high intelligence and a political charisma that gained him the confidence of the nation. Like Churchill, to whom he has been compared, Pitt harnessed the vitality and emotions of the country, infusing England with his vibrant spirit of patriotism and courage, with his vision of victory and the creation of a global empire.

William Pitt was born on November 15, 1708, the younger son of Robert and Harriet Villiers Pitt, daughter of Viscount Grandison. His grandfather was the famous Governor Pitt of Madras—better known as "Diamond Pitt"—from whom he likely inherited the passionate, almost unbalanced, nature that so bewildered and intimidated the political world. At the age of eleven, he proceeded to Eton and in 1727, to Trinity College, Oxford which he left after only a year for the University of Utrecht, where he spent some months studying law but not seriously preparing for a professional career. In 1731, his uncle, Lord Cobham, secured for him a commission in the King's regiment of horse, while in 1733, he made an extended grand tour abroad—including visits to Switzerland and France—returning to England the following year. Pitt's political career began in 1735 with his election to the family borough of Old Sarum—a seat he held until 1747 when he was returned for Seaford. (After that, he sat for Aldborough, 1754–1756; Okehampton, 1756–1757; and for Bath, 1757–1766.) Pitt originally entered Parliament as a member of Lord Cobham's "Boy patriots"—that family based circle of opposition Whigs intent on challenging Walpolean supremacy.[8] It was amidst their ranks that Pitt first gained attention through his fiery denunciations of George II's pro-German policies—attacks which deeply offended the king and hence effectively dashed his prospects of imminent political advancement. In 1737, Pitt linked up with the reversionary interest by becoming Groom of the Chamber to Frederick, Prince of Wales thereby completing his break with the Court. As key opposition speaker, Pitt was to prove instrumental in Walpole's eventual resignation (1742) and in fact sat on the committee which investigated the latter's conduct while in power.[9] Failing to secure office after the fall of Walpole, Pitt spent the next few years in continuing opposition—now to the Carteret connection, Walpole's successors—whom he accused of subservience to Hanoverian interests and neglecting Britain's objectives overseas. Overwhelmed by political pressure, Carteret resigned in 1744. His departure prompted intense negotiations between the Pelham faction and the Crown—negotiations which led to a reconstructed ministry but again, without provision for Pitt whose inclusion was resolutely vetoed by the king. It was only under compulsion—when the Pelhams resigned *en masse*—that George II was compelled to acquiesce in a post for Pitt, first as Vice Treasurer, then shortly afterwards, as Paymaster of the Forces (1746).[10]

Though Pitt's qualities had taken time to emerge, there was an earnestness behind his ambition and confidence in his oratory which, with his courage and determination, clearly proved compelling. Paymaster for nine years, Pitt made constructive use of his office, establishing close contacts with British agents abroad, acquainting himself with French colonial operations and launching new bills for the punishment of mutiny and desertion. In addition, ostentatiously refusing the customary benefits of office, Pitt acquired a unique reputation for disinterestedness among his countrymen that hastened his rise in prestige and would prove a vital element in his growing political appeal.

Until Pelham's death in 1754, Pitt generally supported the government, despite occasionally speaking out against attempted reductions in the navy, which he regarded as the key to Britain's colonial supremacy and against expensive commitments abroad. But by 1755, as promotion eluded him, Pitt again became restive, re-entering the ranks of the opposition once more in alliance with Leicester House[11]—a move which duly prompted his dismissal from office. Only the outbreak of war against France, amidst domestic political upheavals, gave Pitt the opportunity to prove his administrative and strategic flair. Thus in November 1756, after intensive negotiations, Pitt became Secretary of State in a ministry headed by the Duke of Devonshire. He was dismissed the following April, but returned to office in June 1757, again Secretary of State with Newcastle appointed First Lord of the Treasury.

Although the war had begun badly for Britain—successive defeats in 1757–1757 revealing the need for a coherent strategy—under Pitt's direction, the tide gradually turned, victory following victory, until by 1761, Britain's dominance over France in their contest for Empire was securely established. Probably the major achievement of the Pitt–Newcastle coalition was to revitalize British military planning: to clarify the objectives of the war and to evolve a global strategy that placed these objectives into a viable balance, effecting a coordination of means and goals. Refining and developing the experience of earlier Anglo-French wars, Pitt—in collaboration with military/naval advisers—framed an integrated strategy of land/sea cooperation that allowed Britain to keep France occupied in Europe while defeating her overseas.[12] Attention to detail, complete self-confidence and absolute belief in victory all played their part in Pitt's success as war minister and in the political authority he established—authority which visibly lessened following the accession of George III in 1760, the rise of Bute and the spread of wareariness in the nation at large. It was the Cabinet's refusal, in October 1761, to sanction his proposal for a pre-emptive strike against Spain—then joined to France in alliance—which finally prompted him to resign. Although disclaiming all notions of opposition or even a return to power, Pit "remained a key figure in the House and much of the confusion in politics during the next five years was the result of his wayward and incalculable conduct. While acknowledging the right of the Crown to choose its ministers, he would not support the measures of the king; neither would he join wholeheartedly in opposing them."[13] Such was the case during the debates on the peace preliminaries in December 1762, which he criticized bitterly but not in alliance with the Newcastle Whigs, during the negotiations in August 1763 for a new administration—where he proved unpredictable and evasive—and in the debates on general warrants (1764) where again he displayed that remoteness from reality so frequently remarked upon by contemporaries. At all times, Pitt was determined, if he were to resume office, to do so on his own terms. Yet when, in July 1766, he was granted the unconditional direction of affairs as Earl of Chatham, he soon collapsed, incapacitated by erratic infirmities, his continental policy unattained, his American policy in disarray, his ministry lacking stability and direction.

Resigning at last in October 1768, Pitt's health improved somewhat and he became more active politically, speaking in virtually every one of the twenty-two debates in the parliamentary sessions of 1770–1771, ranging from such critical issues as the Falkland crisis, Corsica, the East India Company to the American problem. His initial defense of colonial rights, however tentative, made him a hero in America, with statues raised in his honour, though it is clear that he distanced himself from the colonists after their defiance of the Mutiny Act, which eventually left the initiative in America to others who failed him badly.[14] In fact, recent research has shown that for propaganda purposes, colonial supporters were producing altered reports of Chatham's speeches, representing him as more pro-American than he actually was; certainly his attitude towards the colonists in the 1770's was much more complex and less consistent than the printed version of his speeches would suggest.[15] Moreover, his distinction between internal and external taxes was logically and legally untenable, virtually impossible to maintain in practice,[16] while his belief in British parliamentary supremacy over America, from which he never deviated, would have rendered conciliation with the colonies impossible in any case.[17] Essentially, Chatham's views on empire remained rooted in the old colonial system: he failed to understand the growth of American confidence, self-determination and political self-sufficiency and that consequently, a new framework of imperial governance was inevitable; neither could he acknowledge that America, in the process of becoming a nation, must sooner or later aspire to independence. To accept *that*, he would as soon, he declared, swallow trans-substantiation.[18]

The last years of Chatham's life were arguably tragic ones, twilight years of frustration and failure, marked by growing political isolation, mental illness and physical decay. He gave his last speech in the House of Lords in April 1778—in opposition to the Duke of Richmond's motion to grant American independence—a rambling, incoherent performance at the end of which he collapsed and had to be carried out. Conveyed to Hayes, his country seat, he rallied briefly but soon suffered a relapse and died on May 11. He was buried in Westminster Abbey with fitting pomp.

Chatham's career is unique in our political annals, not only in terms of his example and achievements, but also because—despite his renown, he belonged to no organized faction or party united by a common program or ideology. From 1735, he was connected with different groups—the Cobhamites, the Grenvilles, Leicester House, the Newcastle and Rockingham Whigs—but never for long. Always he returned to that position of independence that was a central feature of his political creed; what made him distinctive and gave him mystique. Political management invariably calls for compromise and tact, the qualities of conciliation for which Chatham had neither aptitude nor taste. Tempermentally an outsider, he possessed a lofty sense of destiny that made him impatient with mediocrity and scornful of partisan politics. The raising of British power and prestige, at all times was Chatham's dominant ambition; the attainment of that ambition against all odds, the true measure of his greatness. Herein also lies the explanation both for his contemporary fame and for his historical reputation.

NOTES

1. F. O'Gorman, *The Rise of Party in England: the Rockingham Whigs, 1760–1782* (London, 1975), p. 73.

2. M. Peters, *Pitt and Popularity: the Patriot Minister and London Opinion during the Seven Years War* (London, 1980), p. 100. cf. *The Conduct of a RT. Honorable gentleman resigning the Seals of his office, justified by facts and upon the principles of the British Constitution* (London, 1761), pp. 33–55.

3. IBID, ch. IX.

4. R. Middleton, *The Bells of Victory: the Pitt-Newcastle Ministry and the Conduct of the Seven Years War, 1757–1762* (Cambridge, 1985).

5. cf. J. Brewer, *The Sinews of Power* (New York, 1989); K. W. Schweizer, *England, Prussia and the Seven Years War* (Lewiston, NY, 1989).

6. Middleton, pp. 8–25.

7. K. W. Schweizer, "An unpublished Parliamentary Speech by the Elder Pitt, 9 December 1761", *Historical Research*, vol. 64, nr. 153 (Feb. 1991), pp. 92–105.

8. Lord Rosebery, *Chatham: His Early Life and Connections* (London, 1910), pp. 130–132.

9. P. D. Brown, *William Pitt: Earl of Chatham* (London, 1978), p. 57.

10. J. Owen, *The Rise of the Pelhams* (London, 1957), pp. 295–302.

11. James, Earl Waldegrave, *Memoirs from 1754 to 1758* (London, 1821), pp. 31–40.

12. K. W. Schweizer, *Frederick the Great, William Pitt and Lord Bute: Anglo-Prussian Relations 1756–1763* (New York, 1991), pp. 96–102.

13. L. Namier and J. Brooke eds., *The History of Parliament: The House of Commons, 1754–1790* (London, 1964), II, p. 295.

14. K. Perry, *British Politics and the American Revolution* (New York, 1990), p. 45 ff.

15. I. Christie, "William Pitt and American taxation", *Studies in Burke and His Times*, vol. 17 (1976), pp. 167–179; J. Sainsbury. "The Pro-Americans of London, 1769–1782", *William and Mary Quarterly*, vol. 35 (1978), pp. 423–454.

16. P. Langford, "Old Whigs, Old Tories and the American Revolution", *Journal of Imperial and Commonwealth History* (1980), pp. 115–116.

17. J.G.A. Pocock ed. *Three British Revolutions: 1641, 1688, 1776* (Princeton, 1980), p. 276.

18. H. von Thal ed. *The Prime Ministers* (London, 1974), p. 153.

Chronology of Significant Events in the Life of William Pitt

1708	15 November	William Pitt born in London, the second son of Robert and Harriet (nee Villiers) Pitt.
1718	September	Entered Eton.
1726	10 January	Admitted "Gentleman Commoner" at Trinity College, Oxford.
1727	20 May	Father died and William left Oxford in October.
1728	January	Proceeded to University of Utrecht.
1731	9 February	Secured commission in the King's Regiment of Horse through his uncle Lord Cobham.
1733	January	Made extended Grand Tour abroad.
1735	18 February	Elected MP for Old Sarum and joined the opposition to Robert Walpole as part of the Cobham connection.
	22 April	Delivered maiden speech in Commons in support of a Place Bill.
1736	29 April	Made abrasive speech on the marriage of the Prince of Wales which infuriated Walpole and led to loss of Pitt's commission.
1737	September	Became Groom of Chamber to Frederick Prince of Wales as well as his Commons spokesman.
1739	14 January	Convention of the Pardo to settle Anglo-Spanish disputes over the Asiento trade and quarrels over English smuggling in Spanish America.

	8 March	Address on Convention with Spain against opposition of Pitt and followers who demanded immediate war with Spain.
	19 October	British declaration of war against Spain.
1740	20 October	Death of Charles VI of Austria and succession of Maria Theresa.
	16 December	Frederick II of Prussia invaded Saxony igniting the War of the Austrian Succession.
1741	8 April	Parliament agrees to support Austria against Prussia and her ally France.
1742	11 February	Resignation of Sir Robert Walpole.
	16 February	New ministry formed, including Earl of Wilmington as 1st. Lord of the Treasury, Carteret as Secretary of State (North) and Newcastle as Secretary of State (South).
1743	16 June	British victory over the French at Dettingen.
	July	Death of Wilmington.
	27 August	Henry Pelham appointed 1st. Lord of the Treasury.
1744	29 March	Britain formally declared war against France.
	May to October	Pitt ill at Bath.
	11 August	Pitt inherited £10,000 from the Duchess of Marlborough for his earlier opposition to Walpole.
	24 November	Carteret forced to resign; Duke of Newcastle and Henry Pelham remodelled government but excluded Pitt.
1745	23 January	Pitt spoke in support of war in Europe, a move calculated to win office.
1746	14 February	Appointed Vice Treasurer of Ireland.
	6 May	Appointed Paymaster General.
1747	30 June	Elected MP for Seaford.
1748	7 October	Peace of Aix-la-Chapelle ends War of Austrian Succession.
1751	20 March	Death of Frederick, Prince of Wales, creating consternation among opposition.
1753	May to March 1754	Recurrent breakdown in health; spent much of his time at Tunbridge Wells and Bath.
1754	6 March	Death of Henry Pelham.
	23 March	New government formed but Pitt denied a place.
	April	Elected MP for Aldborough.

	16 November	Married Lady Hester Grenville.
1755	June	Reopened negotiations with Leicester House opposition.
	20 November	Dismissed as Paymaster General.
	November	Birth of elder daughter Hester.
1756	16 January	Westminster Convention between Britain and Prussia—first stage of the so-called "Diplomatic Revolution"—completed when France allied with Austria (May 1, 1756).
	April	Pitt bought Hayes, his country seat in Kent.
	17 May	Britain declared war on France.
	29 August	Prussia invaded Saxony, beginning the Seven Years War.
	10 October	Birth of eldest son John.
	11 November	Resignation of Newcastle after serious reverses in the war with France.
	15 November	Pitt appointed Secretary of State (South) in reconstituted ministry headed by the Duke of Devonshire.
	11 December	Elected MP for Okehampton.
1757	6 April	Dismissed from office.
	8 June	Passing of Militia Act sponsored by Pitt.
	29 June	New ministry formed after intensive negotiations with Pitt as Secretary of State (South) and Newcastle as 1st. Lord of the Treasury.
	9 July	Elected MP for Bath.
1758	April	Birth of second daughter Harriet.
1759	23 May	Birth of second son William.
	18 September	British forces capture Quebec from the French.
1760	25 October	Death of George II and succession of his grandson George III. Pitt and Newcastle are retained as leaders of ministry despite expectations to the contrary.
1761	24 April	Birth of youngest son James Charles.
	15 August	Third Family Compact between France and Spain obliging the latter to support France if no peace is reached by May 1762.
	18 September	Cabinet rejected Pitt's arguments in favour of immediate war with Spain.

	5 October	Resigned office after disagreement with Cabinet on Spanish issue.
	6 October	Accepted a pension of £3000 per annum and a peerage for his wife.
1762	9 December	Attacked provisions of proposed peace treaty with France in Commons speech lasting three and a half hours.
1763	25 August	Entered into unsuccessful negotiations with the King for a return to office.
1765	February	Inherited Burton Pynsent in Somersetshire.
	16 May	Approached by Cumberland on behalf of George III to negotiate a new ministry to replace the Grenville administration.
	19 to 23 June	Various audiences with King to settle details of new government.
	25 June	Negotiations fail because of Temple's refusal to accept office in Pitt's administration.
1766	14 January	Delivered great speech against Stamp Act.
	12 July	Rockingham dismissed and Pitt elevated to the Lords as Earl of Chatham; forms new ministry as Lord Privy Seal; Duke of Grafton appointed 1st. Lord of the Treasury; Charles Townshend named Chancellor of the Exchequer.
1767	February to March	Breakdown in health.
	13 May	Townshend duties passed by Parliament.
1768	14 October	Resigned office because of continued ill health.
1770	April	Partial repeal of Townshend duties but those on tea retained.
1773	16 December	Boston Tea Party.
1774	28 March	Passage of Coercive Acts against Massachusetts which closed Boston Harbour and quartered troops in Boston.
	5 September to 26 October	Meeting of first Continental Congress in Philadelphia.
1775	20 January	Chatham's resolution for recall of troops from Boston defeated.
	1 February	Provisional bill for settling troubles in America overwhelmingly rejected.

	19 April	American Revolution began in Massachusetts with defeat of British troops by colonial forces at Lexington and Concord.
	10 May	Second Continental Congress at Philadelphia.
1776	4 July	American Declaration of Independence.
1777	30 May	Rejection of Chatham's motion to stop hostilities in America.
1778	7 April	Last speech in the Lords.
	11 May	Death.
	9 June	Buried in Westminster Cathedral.

WILLIAM PITT, EARL OF CHATHAM
1708–1778
A Bibliography

I. Unpublished Personal Papers

A. GREAT BRITAIN

The National Register of Archives, Quality Court, Chancery Lane, London WC2A 1HP, has detailed catalogues of most of the following collections as well as information about conditions of access to papers remaining in private possession. Privately owned collections of documents that have been deposited on loan by their owners in libraries, record offices or other public facilities are normally available for research without restriction. Special conditions may, however, apply and all enquiries should be addressed to the institutions concerned. A microfiche index covering the more important but not all the relevant collections has been published by Chadwyck-Healey Ltd., entitled *National Inventory of Documentary Sources in the United Kingdom* and is available in most larger university libraries. The Royal Commission on Historical Manuscripts has also published a valuable guide to the current location of manuscript collections originally reviewed in the Commission's printed Reports entitled *Guide to the Locations of Collections described in the Reports and Calendar Series 1870–1980*, London, 1982.

Aberystwyth

1. National Library of Wales, Aberystwyth, Dyfed SY 23 3BU

   (a) NLW9669E—Anecdotes of Lord Chatham in the "Commonplace Book of Thomas Salusbury".

(b) NLW11980–1E—Autograph in Autograph Album.

Bakewell

2. Chatsworth, Bakewell, Derbyshire DE4 1PN

(Chatsworth manuscripts) about 45 letters from William Pitt to William Cavendish, 4th. Duke of Devonshire, 1756–1763.

Bedford

3. Bedford County Record Office, County Hall, Bedford MK42 9AP

(Lucas Archive) Reference to Pitt's visit to West Park in letter from Jemima Marchioness Grey to Mary Gregory, 25 July 1754 (L30/9a/2). Report on Chatham's House of Lords Speech 30 May 1777 on motion for stopping hostilities in North America in letter from Lord Polwarth to his wife, 31 May 1777 (L30/11/151/35). Pitt is also one of the writers of letters in information files on Spain (129/342) kept by Lord Grantham as ambassador to Madrid in 1771.

Bury St. Edmunds

4. West Suffolk Record Office, Raingate St., Bury St. Edmunds IP33 1RX
   (a) (Grafton Papers) An extensive collection of correspondence between Pitt and the 3rd. Duke of Grafton, 1762–1777, the most important of which have been reprinted in William Anson ed. *Autobiography and political correspondence of Augustus Henry, Third Duke of Grafton* (London, 1898).
   (b) (Hervey Papers) numerous official and private letters from Pitt as Secretary of State to the 2nd. Earl of Bristol, ambassador in Turin (1755–1758) and Madrid (1758–1761) H.A. 507/7/1–13.

Bute, Isle of

5. Mount Stuart, Isle of Bute, Scotland

(Bute Manuscripts) about 65 letters from Pitt to Bute 1756–1762; also copies of several letters from Bute to Pitt, 1761. (Loudoun Papers) Royal warrant to Pitt, Paymaster to allow Loudoun his expenses during the rebellion, 1750.

Cambridge

6. Cambridge University Library, West Road, Cambridge CB2 1RH

Edward Harley, Parliamentary Diary, 1734–1751 (Add. G851)—a useful source of Pitt's early speeches.

Carlisle

7. Cumbria Record Office, The Castle, Carlisle, Cumbria CA3 8UR

(Lonsdale Archive) Letters from Pitt to Sir James Lowther, 1760 (D/Lons/LI/1/68a).

Chelmsford

8. Essex Record Office, County Hall, Chelmsford CM1 1LX

(Sir John Griffin-Griffin, Lord Braybrooke Correspondence) A bundle of letters between Pitt and Sir John Griffin-Griffin, 1753–1769 (D.DBY. C8, 9).

Dorchester

9. Dorset County Record Office, Bridport Road, Dorchester DT1 1RP

(a) Ryder of Remptone estate archive) Out-letter book of John Calcraft, notes several letters from Pitt, 1746.

(b) Out-letter book of Henry Fox, 3 letters from Pitt, 1746–1748 concerning war office business.

Edinburgh

10. National Library of Scotland, George IV Bridge, Edinburgh EH1 1EW

(a) (Liston Papers) Copies of official/diplomatic correspondence between Pitt and Sir Robert Liston, 1757. NLS, MS.5528.

(b) (Durdans Papers) Typescript copies of letters from Chatham and Lady Chatham to Ann Pitt, 1730–1768. NLS. MS.10224.

11. National Register of Archives, Register House, Charlotte Square, Edinburgh EH2 4DF

(a) (Adam of Blair-Adam Manuscripts) Letter from William Adam (1775) to his parents discussing Chatham's motion to withdraw British forces from Boston and other speeches in Parliament.

(b) (James Grant Papers) Correspondence of James Grant, governor of East Florida, with Pitt (1757–1759) concerning military operations in that area.

12. Scottish Record Office, General Register House, Edinburgh EH1 3YY

(a) (Kinlock of Gourdie family records) Letter from Chatham to the House of Lords (1776).

(b) (Dalhousie Muniments) Duplicate letter from Pitt to Brigadier Forbes instructing the dispatch of Captain Alexander Mackintosh to Halifax to report on the state of Louisiana (1758); numerous letters from General Forbes to Pitt reporting on conduct of campaign against Fort Duquesne.

(c) (Fetteresso Papers) Copy of letter from Pitt to Lord Loudoun (1757).

(d) (Hume of Marchmont Muniments) Letter from William Pitt to Lord Polwarth (c.1737–1738).

(e) (North Berwick Muniments) Letter from Pitt to Sir Hew Hamilton-Dalrymple (1747).

(f) (Baron Polwarth Papers) Letters between various correspondents reporting on Pitt's speeches (1754–1766). An important supplement to the available printed sources.

13. Edinburgh University Library, Special Collections, George Square, Edinburgh EH8 9LJ

(Misc. Manuscripts) one letter to and from Robert Clark (1766) Mis. MSS. 388.

Exeter

14. City Library, Exeter, Devon EX4 3PQ

(Cathcart Papers) A copy of Chatham's plan (1775) for settling American affairs.

Hertford

15. Hertfordshire County Record Office, County Hall, Hertford SG13 8DE

(Panshanger Collection) 3 letters from Pitt to Lord Cowper, 15 January 1761, 6 September 1757, 16 October 1759 (D/EP F249; D/EP F267; D/EP F268).

Iden Green

16. Mill Street House, Iden Green, Kent

(Weston Papers) Private family papers held by Dr. John Weston-Underwood. Includes copies of Pitt's correspondence with assorted diplomats (1757–1760).

Ipswich

17. Suffolk Record Office, Gatacre Road, Ipswich, Suffolk IP1 2LQ

(Barrington Collection) 1 letter from Lord Barrington to Pitt, 12 July 1766 (HA 174: 1026/107). (Letterbook, 1766–1775) 17 letters from Pitt to Barrington on army business, patronage and personal matters, 1758–1768 (HA 174: 1026/112/47–63).

Leeds

18. Public Library, Archives Department, Leeds LS7 3AP

(Cathcart Papers) Copy of Lord Chatham's plan for settling Anglo-American differences and reasserting the sovereignity of Great Britain over her colonies (1775).

London

19. British Library, Department of Manuscripts, Great Russell Street, London WC1B 3DG

  (a) Add. MSS. 5823 (Cole Collection) Epigrams on Pitt (1766) with printed letters from him to Mr. Sayre (1778).

  (b) Add. MSS. 6309. Account of Pitt's funeral, 10 June 1778.

  (c) Add. MSS. 6807–6810, 6817, 6821, 6833. Correspondence with Andrew Mitchell, British ambassador to Prussia (1756–1766). Add. MSS. 6814, 6816–6818, 6830. Letters from Pitt to James Porter (1757–1760). Add. MSS. 6817. Correspondence with Lord Bristol (1759–1760). Add. MSS. 6818. Correspondence with Sir James Grey, envoy to Naples (1759–1760). Add. MSS. 6819.

Letters between Pitt, François de Bussy and Duc de Choiseul (1761).

(d) Add. MSS. 9344 (Misc. manuscripts) Letters to George Jackson (1764–1774).

(e) Add. MSS. 21506 (Original letters and autographs) Letter to Lord Exeter (1758).

(f) Add. MSS. 22626 (original letters) 2 letters from Pitt to the Honourable G. Berkeley and Lady Suffolk (1736, 1741).

(g) Add. MSS. 26889 (William Taylor How Correspondence) Several letters from Pitt to T. Hollis and W. T. How (1762–1765).

(h) Add. MSS. 30877 (Wilkes Papers) 2 letters from Pitt to John Wilkes (1757, 1759).

(i) Add. MSS. 32365 (Drawings and Sketches) 18th. century caricatures of Pitt.

(j) Add. MSS. 32711–32965 (Newcastle Papers) Pitt's correspondence with Newcastle (1747–1765). Add. MSS. 32871, 32897, 32899, 32912, 32921. Correspondence with Lord Hardwicke (1757–1761). (copies) Add. MSS. 32878, 32880. Copies of Pitt's letters to Holdernesse (1758). Add. MSS. 32882, 32926, 32928. Correspondence with Lord Bristol (1758–1761). Add. MSS. 32887. 2 letters to J. West (1759). Add. MSS. 32895, 32902. 2 letters to Baron Munchhausen (1759–1760). Add. MSS. 32923, 32928. Copies of Pitt's correspondence with Hans Stanley concerning the peace negotiations with France (1761). Add. MSS. 33069. 2 letters to the Duchess of Newcastle (1765). Add. MSS. 32973, 32974, 32977. Accounts of conversations between Pitt, Grafton and Rockingham (1766).

(k) Add. MSS. 34412 (Auckland Papers) Copies of Pitt's correspondence with Sir Benjamin Keene concerning Gibraltar (1757).

(l) Add. MSS. 35192 (Bridport Papers) 8 letters to Admiral Alexander Hood (1773–1777).

(m) Add. MSS. 35353, 35423 (Hardwicke Papers) Pitt's correspondence with Lord Hardwicke (1754–1763). Add. MSS. 35417, 35418, 35419, 35422. Copies of Pitt's correspondence with Newcastle (1758–1763). Add. MSS. 35352. 2 letters to Lord Royston (1759).

(n) Add. MSS. 35503, 36123, 36131. Warrants signed by Pitt as Secretary of State (1757–1761).

(o) Add. MSS. 36796 (Register of Bute Correspondence) About 30 letters from Pitt to Bute are listed; the originals of these are at Mount Stuart, Isle of Bute.

(p) Add. MSS. 36806 (Mount Stuart Papers) Correspondence with Benjamin Keene, envoy to Madrid (1757). Add. MSS. 36807. Correspondence with Lord Bristol (1758–1761). (Copies) 1 letter from Pitt to Chevalier Abreu (1759). 1 letter from Abreu to Pitt (1761).

(q) Add. MSS. 36995 (Hodgson Papers) 11 letters from Pitt to General Hodgson (1761).

(r) Add. MSS. 38197, 38333 (Liverpool Papers) Copies of Pitt's official correspondence with Bussy, Choiseul and Hans Stanley (1761). Add. MSS. 38305. Correspondence with Charles Jenkinson (1765–1766). Add. MSS. 38762. Proceedings in Commons relating to the payment of Pitt's debts.

(s) Add. MSS. 40760 (Francis Papers) Pitt's dispatches to Lord Kinnoul, British ambassador to Lisbon (1760). Add. MSS. 40763. 2 Pitt letters, with replies, to Sir Philip Francis (1770).

(t) Add. MSS. 41355 (Martin Papers) Account by S. Johnson of Pitt's altercation with Sir Robert Walpole (1741). Add. MSS. 41356. Account of negotiations with Pitt preceding the Pitt-Devonshire ministry (1756). Add. MSS. 41357. Papers relating to supposed negotiations with Bute for forming a ministry (1778).

(u) Add. MSS. 42084 (Grenville Papers) Pitt's correspondence with George Grenville (1766). Add. MSS. 42087. Correspondence with Lord Temple (1769–1777). The majority printed by Smith, *The Grenville Papers*.

(v) Add.MSS. 43439, 43440 (Keene Papers) Pitt's correspondence (mostly copies) with Sir Benjamin Keene (1756–1757).

(w) Add. MSS. 43771 (Chatham Papers) Correspondence of John Calcraft with Pitt and Countess of Chatham (1746–1772). There are 30 letters from Pitt and 16 from Lady Chatham, written on Pitt's behalf during his bouts of illness; also 24 drafts or copies of memos to Pitt from Calcraft concentrated in the years 1768 to 1772. The correspondence deals mainly with parliamentary and political affairs, especially the widening tension between the government and the city of London.

(x) ADD. MSS. 46196 (Misc. Papers) Correspondence with Lord Rollo (1761).

(y) Add. MSS. 47577 (Fox Papers) Poem on Pitt by Charles James Fox (1764).

(z) Add. MSS. 47896 (Pitt Funeral Drawings) Drawings of the banners for Chatham's funeral (1778), probably the work of Thomas Sharpe, heraldic painter, whose ledgers are now in the Guildhall Library (MS 456 1+2).

(aa) Add. MSS. 57830 (Grenville Papers) Correspondence of Pitt, as Secretary of State, with Hans Stanley, May through September, 1761. (copies) The originals of these are in the Public Record Office S.P.F. 78/251.

(bb) Add. MSS. 57831. Correspondence of Pitt with Duc de Choiseul (1761). (copies)

(cc) Add. MSS. 59484 (Pitt Family Papers) Correspondence and papers of Francis Ayscough on the political affairs of Frederick, Prince of Wales (1747–1754), containing numerous references to Pitt.

(dd) Add. MSS. 59485. Several Pitt letters scattered throughout the general correspondence.

(ee) Add. MSS. 61668 (Blenheim Papers) 1 letter from Pitt to Sarah, Duchess of Marlborough (1758).

(ff) Eg. 929 (Navy Papers) 1 letter from Halifax to Pitt (1758).

(gg) Eg. 1955 (Warburton Papers) 7 letters from Pitt to Dr. Warburton (1759–1763).

(hh) Eg. 3432 (Holdernesse Papers) Correspondence with Lord Holdernesse (1755–1761). Eg. 3432. Several letters to Lord Barrington (1757). Eg. 3430. Copy of minutes to Newcastle (1760). Eg. 3458. Correspondence with Duc de Choiseul (1761). (copies).

(ii) (Stowe Manuscripts) Hanbury-Williams Papers / 263. Copies of Pitt's correspondence with Sir Benjamin Keene (1757).

20. House of Lords Record Office, House of Lords, London SW1A 0PW

Manuscript Minutes of the House of Lords—contains vital information on Chatham's speeches after 1766.

21. National Maritime Museum, Greenwich, London SE10 9NF

(Hawke Papers) Extensive official correspondence between Pitt and Hawke. (Letter Books HWK. 10, 11, 13, 14) especially important for the period 1757–1760; also several private letters from the Admiral to Pitt.

REC/7. Hawke to Pitt, September 1757, giving his own account of the failure of the Rochefort expedition. One letter from Molly Hood to Pitt, 17 May 1753 (MKH/50g).

22. Public Record Office, Ruskin Avenue, Kew, Richmond, Surrey TW9 4DU

As Secretary of State for the South, Pitt not only conducted regular correspondence with British envoys in France, Italy, Switzerland, the Iberian Peninsula and Turkey, but he was also responsible for Ireland, the Colonies and the Channel Islands and routinely wrote to and received communications from diplomats in the Northern Department. Consequently Pitt letters and dispatches can be found in the diplomatic records of that Department as well as among the private papers of specific envoys accredited to the Northern Courts.

The chief sources for Pitt's secretarial activities are the relevant documents in State Papers (Foreign), Entry Books (Domestic), Entry Books (Military), the Colonial Office records, War Office correspondence, Admiralty and Treasury records. Particularly notable among these are the following: State Papers (S.P.) Miscell. 75. Original letter appointing Pitt Secretary of State.

S.P. 109 (various) 68–71. Pitt's Précis Books dealing largely with continental affairs but containing also abstracts of letters from British ministers and consuls at numerous European cities.

S.P. (Domestic) Entry Books 230. Copies of Pitt's instructions to the Lords of the Admiralty, Master General of Ordnance and Secretary of War, 31 December 1757 to 21 July 1760.

S.P. (Domestic) 100. Naval Commanders dispatches. Reports and council minutes relating to expedition against Rochefort; also inquiry into the causes of the failure of this expedition, August–September 1757 and plans by Pitt for expeditions against either Rochefort or Bordeaux.

Colonial Office (C.O.) 5. 13–20. Dispatches to and from all the colonial governors. The bulk of these papers date from 1756, the year war broke out with France and Pitt became Secretary of State for the South. These volumes also contain Pitt's correspondence and should be used in combination with volumes 48–64 (Military Correspondence 1756–1763) and volumes 211–215 (Secretary's dispatches 1753–1763). The latter includes Pitt's entry book of letters written to governors, military officers, naval commanders and to various departments of state. "Military Correspondence" constitutes a large body of letters between William Pitt, his successor Lord Egremont, and the generals and admirals serving in North

America and the West Indies. These letters can also be found in the British Library, Add. MSS. 21634.

Treasury Board I (In Letters) 343. William Pitt to the Treasury regarding the claims of the Colonies, 30 August 1750.

372. Letter from Lord Loudoun to Pitt, 25 April 1757.

377. Letter from Lord Loudoun to Pitt, 3 May 1757.

380. Letters from Pitt to the Treasury, 1758.

396. Governor de Lancy to Pitt, 10 August 1759, with various enclosures.

Pitt's period as Paymaster can be studied in Audit Office (A.O.) 3, Accounts, various—containing Pitt's accounts of salaries and contingencies for the armed forces (1746–1755); Treasury 27 (Out Letters)—Paymaster's correspondence with the Treasury on financial matters and Paymaster–General (P.M.G.) 14, Army miscellaneous books.

(Chatham Papers) P.R.O. 30/8. The principal surviving Pitt family archive, comprising 373 bundles in two series, of which the first, bundles 1–100, contain the correspondence and papers of William Pitt, Earl of Chatham and his wife. The collection is arranged as follows: bundles 1–69 contain their personal correspondence; 70–74 are miscellaneous papers; 75–100 are largely political and official in nature, most bearing upon the period 1748–1776. There is a detailed index in the Search Room. The more important items have also been identified in: L. H. Gipson, *A Guide to Manuscripts Relating to the History of the British Empire, 1748–1776* (New York, 1970), pp. 131–138.

(Hoare or Pitt Papers) P.R.O. 30/70. Another section of the Pitt family archive; contains several letters to Pitt.

Note: European Archives

In his five years as Secretary of State, and even into retirement, Pitt had countless meetings with foreign diplomats and their accounts of these sessions, usually written in French, are preserved in the archives of the countries represented. Here the dispatches of Baron Knyphausen, Prussian minister in London from 1756 to 1763, who was on very close terms with Pitt, are particularly useful. These are located in Deutsches-Zentral Archiv, Merseburg, Germany–Class 33 (A–G) and Rep. 96 (321–L). Also interesting, if somewhat biased, are the observations by the French envoy François de Bussy who conducted peace negotiations with Pitt throughout the summer of 1761. See: Archives du ministère des affaires Etrangères, Paris, Correspondance Politique. Angleterre, volumes 441–443.

23. University College, Gower Street, London WC1E 6BT

(Brougham Papers) Contemporary account of Lord Chatham's speech on the American situation, undated.

Maidstone

24. Kent Archive Office, County Hall, Maidstone, Kent ME14 1XQ

(a) (Sackville of Knole Papers) 4 letters from Pitt to the Duke of Dorset on military matters (1759).

(b) (Stanhope Papers) Assorted family correspondence including letters from Pitt to his wife, to Lord and Lady Stanhope and to James Grenville (1757–1778). One volume of correspondence between William Pitt and Thomas Hollis, (including typescript copies), (1757–1772). 2 letters from Pitt to Thomas Pitt of Boconnock (1774 and nd.); S5/c8 includes papers relating to American affairs, the death of Chatham and one original letter from Robert Clive (1759). There is also one folder containing copies of letters from Pitt to George Speke (1770–1776).

(c) (Amherst Papers) Extensive correspondence with Lord Amherst comprising dispatches and official papers mainly relating to military affairs in North America (1758–1762). These have been well indexed.

Manchester

25. John Rylands Library, University of Manchester, Manchester M3 3EH

(English MS 1272) 2 letters from Lady Harriot Pitt to Lord Chatham (1773).

Nottingham

26. Manuscripts Department, Nottingham University, University Park, Nottingham NG7 2RD

(a) (Newcastle–Clumber MSS) 21 letters from Pitt to Lord Lincoln (1761–1768); 1 letter from Pitt to Newcastle (1759). Reference nrs. NeC 4003–4007; 4237–4244; 4246–4247; 4249–4250; 4252–4254; 4259; 4040.

(b) (Portland Collection) 2 letters from Pitt to the 3rd. Duke of Portland (1771).

Oxford

27. Bodleian Library, Broad Street, Oxford OX1 3BG

One letter from Pitt to an unidentified woman (1754). (MS. Eng. lett. c17, ff. 97–98); a letter to Lord Guilford (1754). (MS. North d.7, ff. 10–11); a letter to William Beckford (1770). (MS. Beckford. c84, ff. 11–12); a letter to a Mr. Carr (nd.). (MS. Autogr. b10, nr. 241). Copy of a letter to Pitt from Charles Townshend (1766). (MS. Eng. hist. d.211, ff. 49–50). Account of a speech in Parliament on 14 January 1766. (MS. Eng. lett. c15, ff. 171–173).

Reading

28. Berkshire Record Office, Shire Hall, Reading, Berkshire RG2 9XD

(Neville Papers) Parliamentary Notebooks of Richard Neville Aldworth, D/EN 034/1–24. 24 volumes (1747–1774). Member of the Bedford group, MP from 1747–1774, Aldworth was an astute observer of political events and his diaries contain important eyewitness accounts of Pitt as a parliamentary speaker.

Sheffield

29. Sheffield Central Library, Surrey Street, Sheffield S1 1XZ

(Wentworth Woodhouse Manuscripts) About 50 letters from William Pitt to the 2nd. Marquis of Rockingham (1764–1778).

Stourbridge

30. Hagley Hall, Stourbridge, West Midlands DY9 9LG

(Lyttelton Papers) 4 letters from Pitt to George Lyttelton (1754–1772). Also an important memoir by Lyttelton, "Observations on Mr. Pitt's Letters of the year 1754" and upon Pitt's career in the ensuing years reflecting their declining relationship prior to the reconciliation of 1770; several letters from Pitt to William Henry Lyttelton while the latter was governor of South Carolina and Jamaica (1757–1765).

Taunton

31. Somerset Record Office, Obridge Road, Taunton TA2 7PU

Several letters to Samuel Hood from the Earl of Chatham (1772–1777). DO/AH 61/21

Estate Papers: abstract of Chatham's title to the Burton Pynsent estate. DD/LC 54/9; copy of will of William Pitt, Earl of Chatham and settling of personal estate (1778). DD/GL/88.

Warwick

32. County Record Office, Priory Park, Cape Road, Warwick CV34 4JS

(a) (Sanderson–Miller Papers) 6 letters from Pitt to various correspondents (1753–1755). CR125B/581–586.

(b) (Denbigh Manuscripts) 1 letter from Pitt to the 6th. Earl of Denbigh (1759). CR2017/C330/16. There is also a copy of this letter. 1 letter from Pitt to General Jeffrey Amherst (1760). CR2017/C330/17.

(c) (Newdigate Manuscripts) Sir Roger Newdigate's Political Diary. Newdigate was an independent MP for Oxford from 1751 to 1780 whose detailed notes of debates for the period contain many references to Pitt's major House of Commons speeches: an indispensable source. There are also references to Pitt in the Mordaunt letters. CR1368/vol V.

Winchester

33. Hampshire Record Office, 20 Southgate Street, Winchester SO23 9EF.

(Stanley Papers) Extensive correspondence between Pitt and Hans Stanley, special envoy to Paris (1761). Many, but not all, of these letters have been reprinted in Thackeray, *Earl of Chatham*, vol. II. See nr. 140. A vital source for Pitt's handling of the 1761 peace negotiations with France.

Windsor

34. Royal Archives, Windsor Castle, Berkshire SL4 1NJ

(a) These are numerous Pitt letters to and from George III among the Georgian papers but most of them, if not all, have been published in *The Correspondence of King George III from 1760 to December 1783*, prepared by Sir John Fortescue. See nr. 118.

(b) (Cumberland Papers) Around 30 letters from Pitt to William Augustus, Duke of Cumberland (1746–1765).

Woburn Abbey

35. Woburn Abbey, Woburn, Bedfordshire

(Bedford Archives) Private family papers: apply in writing to Archivist, Bedford Settled Estates, 29A Montague Street, London WC1.

Correspondence of Pitt and John Russell, 4th. Duke of Bedford, mostly printed in: Lord John Russell ed., *The Correspondence of John, Fourth Duke of Bedford* (London, 1842), 3 vols. Also (Woburn MSS. HMC. nr. 8).

B. UNITED STATES OF AMERICA

Ann Arbor

36. William L. Clements Library, University of Michigan, Ann Arbor, Michigan 48109

(a) (Gage Papers) 1 letter by Pitt to Thomas Gage (1761).

(b) (Germain Papers) Letters from Pitt to the 3rd. Earl of Albemarle, Sir Jeffrey Amherst, Thomas Hopson and James Wolfe (1758–1762).

(c) (Grenville Papers) Numerous letters from Pitt to George Grenville (1756–1757). These have been printed in W. J. Smith ed., *The Grenville Papers* (London, 1852), volume I.

(d) (Lacaita–Shelburne Manuscripts) Drafts of speeches and letters to various unidentified correspondents (1766–1774). 1 letter from Pitt to John Calcraft (1765).

(e) (Lyttelton Papers) 1 letter from Pitt to Lt. Governor of Jamaica (1761); 15 letters to William Henry Lyttelton (1756–1760).

(f) (Melville Papers) Extract of a speech (1770).

(g) (Pitt Papers) 8 Pitt letters (1757–1770); a poem, a draft of a speech and several political memoranda (1750–1777).

(h) (Shelburne Papers) volume 37; 3 letters to Earl of Ancram (1758); 9 letters to Lord Anson (1758); 5 letters to General Bligh (1758); 1 letter to Alexander Dury (1758); 15 directives to the Admiralty (1757); 2 letters to Ordnance (1758); 14 letters to Lord Howe (1758); 1 letter to Lord George Sackville (1758); 2 letters to Rear

Admiral Saunders (1758); 6 letters to the Duke of Marlborough (1758). Assorted papers relating to the Belle-Isle expedition (1761). Volume 22; 2 letters to Earl of Harvey; 1 letter to Count de Fuentes (1760); 5 letters to Benjamin Keene (1757). Volume 25; 2 letters to Edward Hay (1759); 2 letters to Earl of Kinnoull (1760). Volume 58; 1 letter to James Delancey (1758); various letters to American governors (1758–1760). Volume 8; 11 letters to Hans Stanley (1761). Volume 153; numerous letters to the Admiralty and Ordnance (1757–1760); also letters to Lord Anson, Lord Barrington and the Duke of Bedford (1758–1759).

Cambridge, Massachusetts

37. Harvard University, Houghton Library, Cambridge, Massachusetts 02138

A small collection of Pitt letters and related political documents (1757–1770).

Durham, North Carolina

38. William R. Perkins Library, Duke University, Durham, North Carolina 27706

(a) (Pitt Papers) i) An outline of the administrative organization, function and personnel of the Board of Treasury compiled from the Chatham Collection in the Public Record Office, London; ii) An undated note in Chatham's hand wishing success for Robert Nugent in a Bristol election; iii) Several letters from Pitt on diplomatic and political affairs.

(b) (John Almon Papers) Correspondence between Almon and John Calcraft throughout which Pitt is prominently mentioned.

New Haven, Connecticut

39. Beinecke Rare Book and Manuscript Library, Yale University, New Haven, Connecticut

(a) (Boswell Collection) Several Pitt letters (1766–1767).

(b) (Osborne Files) Some 20 Pitt letters to various correspondents including the Duke of Bolton, Lady Chatham, the Earl of Home and Sir Benjamin Keene (1733–1772).

(c) (Uncatalogued manuscripts) 67 letters or copies of letters to and from Pitt.

New York

40. New York Public Library, Manuscript Division, 5th. Avenue and 42nd. Street, New York, New York 10018–2788

   (a) (Emmett Collection) 4 letters from Pitt to the Governor of Pennsylvania (1757–1758); 1 letter to the Governor of Connecticut (1757).

   (b) (Montague Collection) 2 commissions signed by Pitt (1760).

San Marino, California

41. Henry E. Huntington Library, 1151 Oxford Road, San Marino, California 91108

   (a) 27 letters from Pitt to George Grenville (1747–1765), (HM31584–31610) and 12 letters to Earl Temple (1754–1774), (HM31611–31622).

   (b) (Loudoun Papers) 21 letters from Pitt to the Earl of Loudoun and other miscellaneous correspondents (1754–1757).

   (c) (Abercromby Collection) Extensive correspondence between Pitt and James Abercromby (1757–1758); also includes assorted documents relating to military affairs in North America.

   (d) (Hastings Collection) Letters from Pitt to various colonial governors (1758); also letters to Viscount Ligonier, Charles Lloyd, James Grenville and Thomas Townshend (1760–1776).

C. OTHER COLLECTIONS

Smaller collections of Pitt letters, sometimes consisting of only one or two letters, are in: Cambridge University Library; Imperial War Museum, London; Pembroke College, Cambridge; Public Record Office of Northern Ireland, Belfast; Boston Public Library; Historical Societies of Illinois, Pennsylvania, Massachusetts, Maine, New York and Rhode Island; John Carter Brown Library, Providence, Rhode Island; The Lewis Walpole Library, Farmington, Connecticut; Library of Congress, Washington, D.C.; Princeton University Library; Rochester University Library; University of Michigan Library; Virginia University Library and the Public Archives, Ottawa, Canada.

II. Published Compilations of Original Papers

A. HISTORICAL MANUSCRIPTS COMMISSION REPORTS

42. *10th. Report* (Weston–Underwood Manuscripts) London, 1885.

Prints 1 letter from Pitt to Benjamin Keene (1757) and 1 letter from Pitt to Bute (1761).

43. *11th. Report* (Townshend Manuscripts) London, 1887.

Prints 1 letter from General Townshend to Pitt (1759) and 1 from Pitt to Townshend (1957).

44. *12th. Report* (Beaufort Manuscripts) London, 1891.

Prints 1 letter from Pitt to Ligonier (1761).

45. *13th. Report* (Fortescue Papers) appendix, London, 1892.

Prints 1 letter from Chatham to R. Berenger (1771).

46. *14th. Report* (Dartmouth Manuscripts) London, 1895.

Prints 2 letters from Pitt to American governors (1758).

47. *Report on the Manuscripts of the Earl of Ancaster*, Dublin, 1907.

Includes 1 letter from Pitt to the Duke of Ancaster (1759).

48. *Diary of the 1st. Earl of Egmont*, 3 vols., London, 1923.

An excellent source for Pitt's proceedings in Parliament (1735–1743).

49. *Report on the Manuscripts of the Marquess of Lothian*, London, 1905.

1 letter from Pitt to Countess of Suffolk (1742).

50. *Report on the Manuscripts of Lord Polwarth*, vol. V, London, 1961.

1 letter from Pitt to Lord Polwarth (nd.) 2 letters from Pitt to the Earl of Marchmont (1744).

51. *Report on the Manuscripts of Mrs. Stopford-Sackville*, vol., London, 1904.

2 letters from Pitt to Lord George Sackville (1757, 1759).

B. OTHER COLLECTIONS

Readers should be aware that, in general, the editorial standards of the nineteenth century tend to fall short of the standards of today. Editions, therefore, should be used with care and checked against the original documents whenever possible.

52. Chatterton, Georgiana, Lady, ed. *Memorials, personal and historical of Admiral Lord Gambier* 2 vols. London, 1861.

Prints 5 letters from Pitt to his cousin John Pitt (1747–57).

53. [Crowley, T.] *Letters and Dissertations on Various Subjects by "Amor Patriae"* London, 1776.

Prints several letters to Pitt by the author (1768–1769).

54. Dickins, Lilian and Stanton, Mary, ed. *An Eighteenth Century Correspondence* London, 1910.

Prints 6 letters from Pitt to Sanderson Miller (1752–1755). Meticulously edited.

55. Edwards, E. A., ed. *The Love Letters of William Pitt* London, 1926.

A selection from the letters between Pitt and Hester Grenville during their engagement. The originals of these are in the Chatham manuscripts, Public Record Office, vols. 5, 7, 8 and 9.

56. Ellis, Henry, ed. *Original letters illustrative of English history* vol. IV, London, 1827.

Prints numerous interesting letters from Pitt to Sir Andrew Mitchell, British ambassador in Prussia during the Seven Years War. Letters cover the period 1756 to 1760.

57. Great Britain, Department of State, Army. *The Report of the General Officers appointed . . . to inquire into the causes of the failure of the late expedition to the coast of France* London, 1758.

Contains copies of Pitt's letters and instructions relating to the seaborne attack on Rochfort. Also prints many of the reports from the commanders of the expedition to Pitt.

58. Grenville, William Wyndham ed. *Letters written by the late Earl of Chatham to his nephew Thomas Pitt (afterwards Lord Camelford) then at Cambridge* London, 1804. 4 London editions appeared in 1804; also New York, 1804; Cambridge, 1805; Göttingen, 1805; 5th. edition London, 1805; Boston, 1811.

Although written in a characteristically stilted style, these letters offer interesting glimpses into Pitt the "private man".

59. Jesse, J. H. ed. *Memoirs of the Life and Reign of King George the Third* 3 vols. London, 1867.

Prints some letters from Thomas Hollis to Pitt.

60. Kimball, G. S. ed. *Correspondence of William Pitt with Colonial Governors* 2 vols. New York, 1900.

Prints dispatches between Pitt and the governors of the American colonies and West Indian Islands as well as between Pitt and leading naval and military commanders. The editor has also supplied admirable notes and an introduction. A vital primary source for Pitt's strategy in North America and the West Indies.

61. Phillimore, Robert, ed. *Memoirs and Correspondence of George, Lord Lyttelton from 1734 to 1773* 2 vols. London, 1845.

Volume one contains 1 letter from Pitt to Thomas Lyttelton (1748) and 1 to William Lyttelton (1748). Volume two includes the following letters from Pitt: 3 to William Lyttelton (1750, 1754); 14 to George Lyttelton (1754–1772) and 1 to Lord Hardwicke (1754) as well as 1 to Thomas Lyttelton (1773).

62. Russell, John, Lord, ed. *The Correspondence of John, 4th. Duke of Bedford* 3 vols. London, 1842–1846.

Well edited, this collection contains important documents relating to the events preceding Pitt's resignation in 1761, the negotiations for the Peace of Paris, the ministerial crises of 1763 and 1765, including numerous letters from Pitt to Bedford.

63. Smith, W. J. ed. *The Grenville Papers* 4 vols. London, 1852.

The most important collection of printed letters apart from the Chatham Correspondence and Kimball. Contains many letters from Pitt to George Grenville and Temple, together with frequent references to him in letters passing between the Grenvilles, their relatives and friends. Especially valuable for the years 1754 to 1759 and 1766 to 1771.

64. Taylor, William Stanhope and Pringle, John Henry, ed. *Correspondence of William Pitt, Earl of Chatham* 4 vols. London, 1838–1840.

Extensive selection of letters from the Chatham papers preserved in the Public Record Office, together with items from the correspondence of John Calcraft and W. G. Hamilton. The volume contains numerous facsimiles of the handwriting and signatures of Chatham's chief correspondents. Indispensable, although the volumes suffer from repeated errors in transcription and dating.

65. Thackeray, Francis ed. *A History of the RT. Honourable William Pitt, Earl of Chatham* 2 vols. London, 1827.

Prints extensive selection of Pitt's correspondence relating to the peace negotiations with France, April to September 1761.

III. Other Works Printing Pitt Letters

66. Barrington, Shute. *The Political Life of William Wildman, Viscount Barrington* London, 1815.

Includes a letter from Barrington to Pitt (1759).

67. Bigham, Clive. *The Prime Ministers of Britain, 1721–1921* London, 1992.

Prints 1 letter from Voltaire to Pitt (1761) and from Frederick II to Pitt (1761).

68. Broadley, A. M. *Chats on Autographs* London, 1910.

Reprints 2 letters from Pitt to Lord Holdernesse (1759).

69. Copeland, Thomas ed. *The Correspondence of Edmund Burke, 1744–1768* vol. I, London, 1958.

Prints letter from Burke to Pitt (1766).

70. Esdaile, Katharine. *Walpole and Chatham* London, 1918.

Prints letter from Clive to Pitt (1759). Also printed in *Correspondence of William Pitt*, I, pp. 387–392.

71. Gibson, Edward. *Pitt: Some Chapters of his Life and Times* London, 1898.

Prints a letter from Chatham to the Rev. E. Wilson, 29 July 1766.

72. Green, Vivian H. "Advice to a fellow Commoner", *Cambridge Review*, LXIX, nr. 678 (Nov. 1947), pp. 150–152.

Prints Pitt the Elder's advice and syllabus for his nephew Thomas Pitt at Cambridge (1754–1757).

73. Hamilton, M. W. ed. *The Papers of Sir William Johnson* 13 vols. Albany, 1921–1962.

Volume II prints 1 letter from General Abercromby to Pitt (1758); volume III prints 1 letter from Sir William Johnson to Pitt (1760) and 2 from Sir Jeffrey Amherst to Pitt (1761).

74. Harris, George. *The Life of Lord Chancellor Hardwicke* 3 vols. London, 1847.

Prints numerous letters from Pitt to Sir George Lyttelton and Lord Hardwicke and their replies (1754–1760).

75. Hollis, Thomas. *The true sentiments of America contained in a collection of letters sent from the House of Representatives of the Province of Massachusetts Bay to several persons of high rank in this kingdom.* London, 1768.

Includes letters to Chatham, Shelburne and others, most of them written by Samuel Adams.

76. *Letter from the Earl of Chatham to Joseph Turner, Oct. 3, 1773, produced in facsimile from the original manuscript in the possession of the Master of Pembroke College* Cambridge, 1906.

77. Maxwell–Lyte, H. C. *A History of Eton College, 1440–1910* London, 1911.

Prints a letter from Pitt to his father (1723).

78. Moore, Thomas. *Memoirs of the Life of the Right Honourable Richard Brinsley Sheridan* London, 1825.

Prints 1 letter from Pitt to Thomas Nuthall (1770).

79. Oswald, James. *Memorials of the Public Life and Character of the Right Honourable James Oswald* Edinburgh, 1825.

Prints a letter from Pitt to Oswald (nd.).

80. Peach, R. E. *The Life and Times of Ralph Allen of Prior Park* London, 1895.

Prints 4 letters from Pitt to Ralph Allen (1757–1763); 5 letters from Allen to Pitt (1957–1763); 1 letter from the Bath corporation to Pitt

(1761) and Pitt's reply. Most of these letters are also reproduced in the same author's *Historic Houses in Bath and their associations* London, 1883.

81. Rodd, Thomas, ed. *Original Letters from Lord Charlemont, the Right Honourable Edmund Burke, William Pitt, Earl of Chatham and many other distinguished noblemen and gentlemen to the Right Honourable Henry Flood* London, 1820.

82. Rosebery, Lord. *Chatham: His early Life and Connections* London, 1910.

Prints many letters from Pitt (1726–1756).

83. Savory, Reginald. *His Britannic Majesty's Army in Germany During the Seven Years War* Oxford, 1966.

Prints excerpt of a letter from Prince Ferdinand to Pitt (1760) and part of one from the Duke of Marlborough to Pitt (1758).

84. Sedgwick, Romney. 'Letters from William Pitt to Lord Bute, 1755–1758' in: *Essays presented to Sir Lewis Namier*, Richard Pares and Allan John Perceval Taylor eds., London, 1956. pp. 108–166.

These letters, preserved among the Bute Papers at Mount Stuart, Isle of Bute, chronicle the gradual estrangement between Bute and Pitt following the formation of the Newcastle-Pitt administration. Valuable for illustrating Pitt's supreme pragmatism in adjusting his principles to the needs of office at the expense of former loyalties and political affiliations.

85. Sedgwick, Romney. "William Pitt and Lord Bute: an intrigue of 1755–1758", *History Today*, VI (1956), pp. 647–654.

Prints extracts of letters from Pitt to Bute (1755–1758), illustrating the alliance and gradual alienation between Pitt and Leicester House, the opposition party centered around the Prince of Wales.

86. Van Alstyne, Richard. "Europe, the Rockingham Whigs and the War for American Independence—Some Documents", *Huntington Library Quarterly*, XXV (1961), pp. 1–28.

Prints letter from Chatham to Rockingham (1778).

87. Whitton, F. E. *Wolfe and North America* Boston, 1929.

Prints a letter from Wolfe to Pit (1759).

88. Wickham–Legg, L. G. ed. *British Diplomatic Instructions Volume 7: France (1745–1789)* London, 1934.

   Valuable as a source of Pitt's diplomatic correspondence as Secretary of State.

89. Willson, Beckles. *The Life and Letters of James Wolfe* London, 1909.

   Prints 6 letters from Wolfe to Pitt (1758–1759); 1 letter from Mrs. Wolfe to Pitt (1759) and the reply, dated 17 January 1760.

IV.   Speeches

The sources for parliamentary debates during Pitt's lifetime fall into three major categories: diaries and notes taken by members of the Houses throughout the proceedings, accounts found in the general political correspondences of the period and reports printed in contemporary magazines, periodicals and pamphlets. Such printed reports were often fragmentary and inaccurate but remained the only published source of parliamentary information until the commencement of regular newspaper coverage of debates in the 1770's. These accounts in turn—subsequently reprinted in the multi-volume collections compiled by Almon, Debrett and Cobbett—must also be treated cautiously. Since reporters (no notes being allowed in Parliament before 1783) were forced to rely heavily on hearsay or memory, their reports, of larger speeches especially, are often highly impressionistic and should be checked against the accounts of firsthand observers whenever possible. Some of these accounts have been published and are listed below; others have remained in manuscript and are noted in section I. On the reporting and publishing of parliamentary debates see: P.D.G. Thomas, "The Beginning of Parliamentary Reporting in Newspapers, 1768–1774", *English Historical Review* 74 (1959), pp. 623–636; F. Siebert, *Freedom of the Press in England, 1476–1776* (Urbana, 1952), pp. 346–354.

The standard sources for Pitt's parliamentary speeches are:

90.   (a) Almon, John. *The Debates and Proceedings of the British House of Commons from 1743 to 1774* 11 vols. London, 1766–1775.

Perhaps the leading political publisher and bookseller of his time, Almon had extensive private sources of information. Indeed, frequently members of Parliament themselves supplied him with speeches. Hence, his work is more reliable than other such compilations though the phrases and arguments attributed to certain speakers, Pitt included, cannot always be accepted verbatim.

  (b) Chandler, Richard. *The History and Proceedings of both Houses of Commons* 14 vols. London, 1742–1743.

Volumes 9–13 reprint many of Pitt's early speeches collected from the major magazines.

  (c) Debrett, John. *The History, Debates and Proceedings of both Houses of Parliament, 1743 to 1774* 7 vols. London, 1792.

  (d) Cobbett, William. *The Parliamentary History of England from the Earliest Period to the Year 1803* 36 vols. London, 1806–1820.

The prefaces of volumes IX, X, XI and XII give helpful descriptions of the sources drawn upon by the editor. It should be noted that Cobbett's *Parliamentary History*, though more generally available in university libraries than Debrett's work, does not provide such complete or accurate reports of the debates. Cobbett neither published his accounts concurrently with parliamentary proceedings nor did he produce wholly accurate, full-length reports of many crucial speeches.

91. Simmons, R. C. and Thomas, P.D.G. eds. *Proceedings and Debates of the British Parliaments Respecting North America, 1754–1783* 6 vols. New York, 1982–1986.

The most authoritative edition for Pitt's addresses relating to North America in the House of Commons and after 1766, the House of Lords.

  (a) Simmons and Thomas, *Proceedings and Debates*, volume I (New York, 1982) assembles Pitt's speeches concerning the Anglo-French conflict in America drawn from a variety of contemporary sources including manuscript material. It incorporates many items (petitions, accounts, addresses, etc.) not printed in the official *Journals* of the two Houses. For a general list of these items as well as available sessional papers not previously published see: Sheila Lambert, *House of Commons Sessional Papers of the Eighteenth Century* (Wilmington, Del., 1975) and F. W. Torrington ed., *House of Lords Sessional Papers, 1641–1805* (Dobbs Ferry, 1972, 1977).

(b) Simmons and Thomas, *Proceedings and Debates*, volume II (New York, 1983) contains Pitt's speeches on the Stamp Act crisis and the Townshend duties.

(c) Simmons and Thomas, *Proceedings and Debates*, volume III, 1768–1773 (New York, 1984) prints Chatham's speeches in the House of Lords on the colonial reaction to the Townshend duties and related British measures.

(d) Simmons and Thomas, *Proceedings and Debates*, volume IV, January–May 1774 (New York, 1985) contains Chatham's speech on the American Quartering Bill, 26 May 1774.

(e) Simmons and Thomas, *Proceedings and Debates*, volume V, June 1774–March 1775 (New York, 1986) prints Chatham's speeches during the Lords Debate on the following subjects: Quebec Bill, 17 June 1774; Motion for an Address to remove the troops from Boston, 20 January 1775; Provisional Acts for settling the trouble in America, 1 February 1775.

(f) Simmons and Thomas, *Proceedings and Debates*, volume VI, April 1775–May 1776 (New York, 1986). Chatham is frequently mentioned but no speeches are recorded as he was absent from late 1775 to 1777 due to illness.

One of Pitt's major speeches in the House of Commons and at least 6 of his speeches in the House of Lords were published as pamphlets. These are listed below in chronological order of speech, not of publication.

92. *The celebrated Speech of a late celebrated Commoner upon the American Stamp Act which was afterwards repealed* London, 1766.

A new corrected edition appeared in 1775. Pitt's speech, delivered on 14 January 1766, was an explicit statement of his imperial philosophy. He acknowledged the right of Parliament to impose an external tax upon the colonies and to regulate their commerce but not to impose direct taxation on those not politically represented. At the same time, he urged that "the sovereign authority of this country over the colonies be asserted in as strong terms as can be devised"—an affirmation of parliamentary authority eventually encapsulated in the Declaratory Act. An important clarification of key aspects of Pitt's speech as reported by contemporary observers has been made by I. R. Christie, "William Pitt and American Taxation", *Studies in Burke and his Times*, 17 (1976), pp. 167–179.

93. *The Speech of Mr. P . . . and several others in a certain august assembly on a late important debate* London, 1766.

94. *The Speech of Mr. Pitt, now Earl of Chatham, upon the Stamp Act, wherein the arguments of Mr. Gr . . . v . . . ille and others in favor of the Act are answered* Dublin, 1768.

95. *Dickinson, John. Letters from a farmer in Pennsylvania, to the inhabitants of the British Colonies regarding the right of taxation and several other important points. To which are added, as an appendix, the speeches of Lord Chatham and Lord Camden, the one upon the Stamp Act, the other on the Declaratory Bill* Dublin, 1768.

96. *The Speeches of the Right Hon. Mr. Pitt, Gen. Conway, George Grenville, Mr. Nugent, etc. in Parliament on Tuesday the 14th. day of January 1766 for and against the repeal of the Stamp Act* Philadelphia, 1766.

97. [John Wilkes]. *The Celebrated Speech of a Celebrated Commoner* Paris, 1766.

98. *An authentic copy of Lord Ch . . . . m's Speech in the House of Lords in England in the debate on the present state of the Nation, November 22, 1770* London, 1770.

A speech supporting the Duke of Richmond's motion for the production of all letters and papers relating to hostilities between Britain and Spain over the Falkland Islands.

99. *The Speech of the Right Hon. the Earl of Chatham in the House of Lords upon reading the amendments in the Quebec bill on Friday, the 17th. of June, 1774* London, 1774.

100. *The Speech of the Right Honourable the Earl of Chatham in the House of Lords, January 20, 1775* London, 1775.

There was a new London edition, a Dublin edition and a Newport, Rhode Island edition, all published in 1775. These differ materially from the edition printed in Philadelphia the same year (see below). The speech relates to Chatham's motion to withdraw British forces from Boston without delay.

101. *The Speech of the Right Hon. the Earl of Chatham in the House of Lords, January 20, 1775, on a motion for an address to His Majesty to give immediate orders for removing his troops from Boston forthwith* Philadelphia, 1775.

The Philadelphia edition also appeared in German translation *Des Hoch Edlen Grafen von Chatham Rede gehalten im Hause der Lords, den 20 sten Jenner, 1775*. Philadelphia, 1775.

102. *Plan offered by the Earl of Chatham to the House of Lords entitled, A provisional Act for the settling of troubles in America and for asserting the supreme legislative authority and superintending power of Great Britain over the Colonies* London, 1775.

A new edition was published in Annapolis the same year. As set forth in a speech on 1 February 1775. Essentially the plan reaffirmed imperial authority in America but made taxation subject to colonial consent. The Crown was to retain its military prerogatives but no troops were to be stationed in America; the Philadelphia Congress was officially recognized while the Admiralty Courts would have their powers reduced and the recently legislated coercive acts were to be repealed. The plan, not likely to have been acceptable to the Americans, was duly dismissed by the Upper House.

103. *Lord Chatham's Speech in the British House of Lords at the opening of the session, 20th, November 1777 on the debate for addressing the throne* np., 1778.

A speech moving for the recall of the British Army from America, conciliation of the colonists and immediate preparations against France and Spain.

104. *A faithful abstract of Lord Chatham's last Speech in Parliament, 7 April 1778, the day he was struck with the illness which terminated in his death* London, 1778.

Speech in opposition to the Duke of Richmond's motion to grant American Independence. Historians are generally agreed that Chatham's melodramatic oratory and appearance mark this occasion as one of the great events in parliamentary history.

Various extracts from the major sources of Pitt's speeches have been collected in:

105. *The Speeches of the Right Honourable the Earl of Chatham with a biographical memoir, introduction and explanatory notes* London, 1848 (and numerous later editions).

Other printed sources and commentaries on Pitt's speeches are to be found in the works listed below.

106. Almon, John. *Anecdotes of the Life of the Rt. Hon. William Pitt, Earl of Chatham* 3 vols. London, 1793.

Prints numerous speeches derived from a variety of contemporary sources, magazines and pamphlets in particular.

107. Bargar, B. D. "Chatham's first debate in the House of Lords", *Journal of Modern History*, XXIX (1957), pp. 361–362.

A candid and lively report of Chatham's maiden speech in the House of Lords on prohibition of grain exports, 11 November 1766, as contained in a letter from Lord Dartmouth to the Earl of Guilford, 13 November 1766. The original is among the North MSS 10, ff. 198–199, Bodleian Library, Oxford.

108. Barker, G.F.R. ed. *Horace Walpole, Memoirs of the Reign of King George III* 4 vols. London, 1894. Reprinted 1970.

There is an earlier edition in 4 volumes, published in 1845, edited by Sir Denis le Marchand. Walpole, in France from September 1765 to April 1766, was absent from most of the important parliamentary sessions of 1765–1766; hence his reports, largely fragmentary, are not firsthand. For that brief period, Fortescue, Ryder and Simmons/Thomas are more reliable authorities.

109. Barnwell, Joseph. "Hon. Charles Garth, MP. The last colonial agent of South Carolina in England and some of his work". *The South Carolina Historical and Genealogical Magazine* 26 (1925), pp. 65–92; 28 (1927), pp. 79–93; 29 (1928), pp. 41–48, 115–132, 212–230, 295–305. Letters to the South Carolina legislature by an intelligent, firsthand observer, containing detailed references to Pitt's parliamentary speeches from 14 January 1766 to 24 April 1766, the date of his last speech in the Commons. It provides a masterly summation of the arguments pro and con regarding the repeal of the Stamp Act.

110. *Boyd, Hugh. Genuine Abstracts from two Speeches of the late Earl of Chatham* London, 1779.

Contains the speeches of 20 January 1775 and 20 November 1777 reported by Boyd, prefaced by an introduction with elaborate description of Pitt's oratory. It appears that the above rendition of the first speech is a mutilated version of an earlier, more complete account sent by the publisher, James Dodsley, to his American counterpart, John Dunlap, in early 1775 who duly published it in pamphlet form in June of that year. On the publication history see: Robert R. Rhea, "Anglo-American

Parliamentary Reporting: A Case Study in Historical Bibliography",
Bibliographical Society of America, Papers, XLIX (1955), pp. 224–
228.

111. Brooke, John ed. Horace *Walpole. Memoirs of King George II* 3
vols. New Haven/London, 1985.

These impeccably edited volumes replace the less scholarly edition
Memoirs of the Reign of George II by Lord Holland, ed. 3 vols. London,
1847. Though Walpole's statements, given his partisan feelings, frequently
require verification in details, as a firsthand observer in Parliament, his
account of debates form a rich depository of parliamentary information
and make him a leading recorder of contemporary political events. The
Memoirs are also notable for their vivid and accurate depiction of Pitt's
oratorical style.

112. Campbell, L. D. ed. *The Miscellaneous Works of Hugh Boyd* vol. I,
London, 1800, pp. 247–249.

Provides an abbreviated version of Chatham's House of Lords speech
on 20 January 1775. For long considered a definitive account but see the
bibliographical analysis and re-evaluation by Rea, "Anglo-American Parliamentary Reporting", pp. 212–229.

113. *Celebrated speeches by Chatham, Burke and Erskine. Selected by a
member of the Philadelphia bar* New York, 1834. Also various later
editions.

114. Charlemont, Lord. *Original Letters to the Right Hon. Henry Flood*
London, 1820.

Useful contemporary references to Pitt's more important speeches.

115. Copeland, Thomas ed. *The Correspondence of Edmund Burke,
1744–1768* vol. I, London, 1958.

A well prepared and carefully annotated edition of all the important
extant letters which Burke sent or received. Volume I has a full report by
Burke of Pitt's important speech against the Stamp Act, delivered on 14
January 1766.

116. Cradock, Joseph. *Literary and Miscellaneous Memoirs.* Edited by J.
B. Nichols. 4 vols. London, 1828.

Provides interesting account of Chatham's speech on 9 January 1770.

117. Egmont, 1st. Earl. *Diary of Viscount Perceval, afterwards First
Earl of Egmont* 3 vols. London, 1920–1923.

Volume II contains informative reports on some of Pitt's early speeches in Parliament.

118. Fortescue, John, Sir ed. *The Correspondence of King George III from 1760 to 1783* 6 vols. London, 1927–1928.

Offers a wealth of reports on debates in both Houses and Pitt's speeches by various correspondents of the king. (Should be supplemented by Lewis Namier, *Additions and Corrections to Sir John Fortescue's Edition of the Correspondence of King George III* London, 1937.)

119. Gipson, L. H. "The Great Debate in the Committee of the whole House of Commons on the Stamp Act as reported by Nathaniel Ryder", *Pennsylvania Magazine of History and Biography*, 86 (1962), pp. 10–41.

Provides a full account of Pitt's speeches on 21 February 1766 during the debate in committee on leave to repeal the Stamp Act supplemented by useful editorial references to other contemporary records of debate.

120. Grattan, Henry. *Memoirs of the Life and Times of.* 5 vols. London, 1839–1846.

Volume I contains a report of Chatham's speech in the Lords on 9 January 1770.

121. *Historical Manuscripts Commission*, Fifth Report, Appendix III. Stopford–Sackville MSS, London, 1904.

Includes reports on Pitt's major speeches (1765–1766) in letters from Lord George Sackville to General Irwin. (The originals of these letters, together with related papers, are now in the William Clements Library, Ann Arbor, Michigan.)

122. Hull, C. H. and Temperley, H. W. V. eds. "Debates on the Declaratory Act and the Repeal of the Stamp Act, 1766", *American Historical Review*, XVII (1911–1912), pp. 563–586.

Prints Pitt's speech on the Declaratory Act, 3 February 1766, based on notes taken by Grey Cooper MP for Rochester. A detailed report on this debate was also made by Charles Garth, agent for the colonies of South Carolina and Maryland, to the three delegates to the Stamp Act Congress from Maryland and is valuable for its summarization of the major constitutional points developed in the debate. See "Stamp Act Papers", *Maryland History Magazine*, V (1911), pp. 282–305.

123. Knollenberg, Bernard. *Franklin, Jonathan Williams and William Pitt: a letter of 21 January 1775* Bloomingdale, Indiana University Library, 1949.

Reproduces and discusses the letter in which Williams reported to an unnamed correspondent on the debate and rejection by the House of Lords of Chatham's motion for withdrawal of the British troops from Boston. Original manuscript is preserved in the Indiana University Library, Bloomington, Indiana.

124. Labaree, L. W. ed. *The Papers of Benjamin Franklin* vol. 13, New Haven, 1959.

Reports Pitt's speeches on the Stamp Act in support of its repeal. (January 1–December 31, 1766).

125. Lewis, W. S. ed. Selected Letters to Horace Walpole New Haven/London, 1973.

Prints letter from Horace Walpole to Richard Bentley, 16 November 1755, describing Pitt's speech in answer to Lyttelton during the Debate on the Address.

126. Lewis, W. S. ed. *The Yale Edition of Horace Walpole's Correspondence* 40 vols. New Haven, 1937–1980.

A superb edition and key source for eighteenth century British political/social history as well as Pitt's parliamentary performance.

127. *Lord Chatham's speeches on the American Revolution* Boston, 1908.

Prints speech on the Stamp Act, 14 January 1766; speech on the bill for quartering troops in North America, 27 May 1774; Lord Chatham's motion to withdraw the troops from Boston, 20 January 1775; Chatham's motion for an Address to the Crown to put a stop to hostilities in America, 30 May 1777.

128. *Lord Chatham's speech in the House of Lords, 20 January 1775, urging the removal of the troops from Boston* Boston, 1886; new edition Boston, 1891.

129. Mantoux, P. *Notes sur les Comptes Rendus du Parlement Anglais aux Archives des Affaires Etrangères* Paris, 1906.

Indicates sources for Pitt's speeches in the French Archives.

130. Morgan, Edmund. *Prologue to Revolution: Sources and Documents on the Stamp Act Crisis, 1764–1766* Chapel Hill, 1959.

Prints Pitt's famous speech of January 1766 arguing that the Stamp Act was ill-judged and deserved immediate repeal (doc. 56). Included also is a report by Charles Garth, agent for Maryland, describing Pitt's observations during the debate on the Declaratory Act, 4 February 1766 (doc. 59b).

131. Mure, William ed. *Selections from the Family Papers preserved at Caldwell. In Two Parts* Glasgow, 1854.

Useful and generally reliable account of Pitt's speeches from 1766 onwards.

132. Niles, H. *Principles and Acts of the Revolution* Baltimore, 1822.

Has three reports of Chatham's speeches but with the wrong dates.

133. Nivernois, Duc de. *Oeuvres Posthumes* 2 vols. Paris, 1807.

Has a report of Pitt's speech on the Peace Preliminaries, 6 December 1762.

134. Parkes, Joseph and Merivale, Herman eds. *Memoirs of Sir Philip Francis* 2 vols. London, 1867.

The Appendix to volume one contains two accounts of Chatham's speeches delivered in the House of Lords in 1770. A not very reliable source.

135. Rogers, J. A. Thorold. *A Complete Collection of the Protests of the Lords* 3 vols. Oxford, 1875.

Volume II prints 5 of Chatham's protests.

136. Quincy, Josiah ed. *Memoir of the Life of Josiah Quincy*, Jun. Boston, 1874 (2nd. edition).

According to Benjamin Franklin, Quincy compiled one of the best accounts of Chatham's motion of 20 January 1775 for the withdrawal of British forces from Boston. See A. H. Smyth ed. *Writings of Benjamin Franklin* New York, 1906. Vol. VI, pp. 445–446.

137. Schweizer, Karl. "An unpublished Parliamentary Speech by the Elder Pitt, 9 December 1761", *Historical Research*, vol. 64, nr. 153 (Feb. 1991), pp. 92–105.

Pitt's famous defense of foreign subsidies and continental commitments based on minutes taken by Charles Jenkinson preserved among the Liverpool Papers (Add. MS 38334, ff. 33–39) in the British Library. Provides the clearest formulation of the strategic principles underlying Pitt's policies during the Seven Years War.

138. Steuart, A. F. ed. *The Last Journals of Horace Walpole during the reign of George III* 2 vols. London, 1910.

Valuable for Chatham's later speeches in the House of Lords.

139. Stevens, B. F. *Facsimiles of MSS in European Archives relating to America, 1773–1783* 25 vols. London, 1889–1898.

Provides numerous reports of Chatham's speeches in French archives.

140. Thackeray, Francis. *A History of the Right Honourable William Pitt, Earl of Chatham* 2 vols. London, 1827.

A rich but sometimes suspect source. Thackeray's version of Pitt's speeches should be collated with other contemporary renditions, such as Walpole's, whenever possible.

141. *The speeches of the Right Honourable the Earl of Chatham in the Houses of Lords and Commons with a biographical memoir, introduction and explanatory notes to the speeches* London, 1848.

142. Thomas, P.D.G. ed. "The Parliamentary Diaries of Nathaniel Ryder, 1764–1767", *Camden Miscellany*, XXIII, London, 1969, pp. 229–351.

Reports of debates based on shorthand notes in the Harrowby MSS, Sandon Hall, Staffordshire. Ryder was MP for Tiverton from 1756 to 1776, with an astute eye for motive, character and detail. Expertly edited, this work is indispensable for Pitt's speeches on the Stamp Act and his role in securing its repeal.

143. Watson, D. ed. "William Baker's account of the Debate on the Repeal of the Stamp Act", *William and Mary Quarterly* XXVI (1969), pp. 259–265.

A letter of William Baker (1743–1824), Rockingham adherent, to an unknown correspondent, containing references to Pitt's speeches during debates (21–24 February 1766) concerning the proposed repeal of the Stamp Act. Original is among the Baker MSS preserved at the Hertfordshire County Record Office.

V. Published Writings of William Pitt

Apart from his published speeches and letters and various unpublished items preserved in the Public Record Office (Chatham Papers), Pitt wrote very little and even the writings that can definitely be attributed to him largely appeared long after his death.

144. *A Letter on superstition by the Right Honourable William Pitt. First printed in the London Journal of 1733* London, 1819.

There was an earlier reprint of 1751, and it was reprinted again in 1820 as a hawker's broadsheet. Further editions appeared in 1867 and 1873 (see below). For the argument that the author of this pamphlet was not William Pitt but James Pitt, see B. Williams, *William Pitt, Earl of Chatham* vol. I (London, 1915), p. 216, note 2.

145. *An Appeal to the justice and interests of the people of Great Britain in the present disputes with America* London, 1774. At least 5 editions.

This pamphlet has been variously attributed to Chatham, Benjamin Franklin and Richard Glover.

146. *Humanity: the only true divinity* Boston, 1867.

Attributed to Pitt by NUC 460.113.

147. *Superstition displayed: being the celebrated letter of William Pitt with an introduction by Austin Holyoke* London, 1873.

148. Smith, W. *The History of the Peloponnesian War* 2 vols. London, 1753.

Contains Pitt's translation of Pericles' last speech.

149. Winans, Ross ed. *Gleanings from Chatham and other authors* Baltimore, 1872.

VI.   Pamphlets Relating to Pitt

Few eighteenth century public figures generated more political commentary, both supportive and critical, than William Pitt. Much of this was richly chronicled in the contemporary press, especially in pamphlet form—pamphlets constituting the major forum for political controversy and debate, catering to a diverse audience, well informed and actively interested in Court, Parliament and beyond. Since, inevitably, the pamphlet literature on Pitt is immense—at least passing reference to the "great Commoner" occurring in virtually every pamphlet published during this period—only those pamphlets are listed in which Pitt is the primary focus of discussion or those providing coverage of issues with which Pitt was directly involved. The pamphlets are grouped according to topic and these are arranged chronologically. Most of the pamphlets referring to Pitt are listed in the *British Library Catalogue* and in Watts, *Bibliotheca Britannica* (London, 1824). For pamphlets published in America, see Charles Evans, *American Bibliography: A Chronological Dictionary of all Books, Pamphlets and Periodical Publications from 1639 to 1820*, 13 vols. (1903); reprint edition (New York, 1941).

The location of pamphlets noted below is the British Library unless otherwise indicated.

DEFENCES OF PITT'S OPPOSITION TO CARTERET'S GERMAN POLICY, 1742–1744

150. Campbell, John. *The case of the opposition impartially stated. By a gentleman of the Inner Temple* London, 1742.

151. Egmont, 2nd. Earl of. *Faction Detected by the evidence of Facts: containing an impartial view of parties at home, and affairs abroad* London, 1743. Various editions.

152. —————. *The English Nation Vindicated from the Calumnies of Foreigners; In Answer to a late pamphlet entitled, Popular Prejudice concerning partiality to the Interests of Hanover* London, 1744.

153. [Hervey, John]. *Miscellaneous Thoughts on the present posture both of our Foreign and Domestic Affairs. Humbly offer'd to the Consideration of the Parliament and the People* London, 1742.

154. *Opposition not Faction: Or, the Rectitude of the Present Parliamentary Opposition to the Present Expensive Measures justified by Reason and Facts. In a letter from Bath to a Member of Parliament* London, 1743.

155. [Pulteney, William]. *A Proper Answer to the Bystander: wherein is shewn that there is no necessity for, but infallible ruin in the maintenance of a large regular (or mercenary) land force in this island* London, 1742.

156. *The Case of the Hanover Forces in the Pay of Great Britain* London, 1742.

Enumerates Pitt's arguments against subsidy treaties and continental commitments.

THE JACOBITE THREAT, 1745

157. *A dissertation on nothing: or, remarks on A Letter to William Pitt wherein is contained nothing* London, 1746.

158. *An epistle to William Pitt, Esq.* London, 1746.

159. [Hervey, Thomas]. *A Letter to William Pitt, concerning the Fifteen New Regiments lately voted by Parliament* London, 1746.

A friendly exposition on Pitt's defence of these regiments.

160. *The Spirit and Principles of the Whigs and Jacobites compared: being the substance of a discourse delivered in Edinburgh, December 1745* London, 1746.

DEVONSHIRE–PITT ADMINISTRATION, 1756–1757

161. *A Letter to the Gentleman of the Common Council by a Citizen and Watchmaker* London, 1756.

Favourably compares opposition leaders, including Pitt, with members of the current administration and urges a coalition between Pitt and Fox.

162. *A New System of Patriot Policy containing the Genuine Recantations of the British Cicero* London, 1756.

An early hostile reassessment of Pitt's career emphasizing his many inconsistencies and questioning the validity of his patriot reputation. Contains effective parodies of Pitt's oratory.

163. *A Political Treatise on the National Humour. In Which the character and conduct of a statesman is generally and impartially considered. Addressed to the RT. Hon. William Pitt, Esq.* London, 1756.

164. [Shebbeare, John]. *A Fifth Letter to the People of England, on the subversion of the Constitution: and, the necessity of its being restored* London, 1757.

165. *The Aequipoise, or the Constitution Balanced* London, 1757.

Defends Pitt against the aspersions of the *Test*.

166. *The Enquiry is not begun! When will it?* London, 1757.

A Broadside deploring Pitt's dismissal from office on 6 April 1757.

167. *The Fatal Consequences which may arise from the want of system in the conduct of public affairs* London, 1756.

Urges Newcastle's resignation and Pitt's accession to office.

168. *The Ministry changed: Or, The clean contrary way. A new Song, To an Old Tune* London, 1756.

Ballad acclaiming Pitt's accession to office.

THE LOSS OF MINORCA AND TRIAL OF
ADMIRAL BYNG

169. *Admiral Byng's Answer to the Friendly Advice, Or the Fox out of the Pit and the Geese In* London, 1756.

   Broadsheet generally supportive of Pitt's stand on the Minorca enquiry.

170. *The Case of the Honourable Admiral Byng, Ingenuously Represented* London, 1757.

171. *A Collection of Several Pamphlets . . . relative to the Case of Admiral Byng* London, 1756.

172. *The Enquiry is not begun! When will it?* London, 1757.

173. *An Exact Copy of a Remarkable Letter from Admiral Byng to the Right Honourable William Pitt* London, 1757.

   Pro Byng but not anti-Pitt.

174. *A Letter to the RT. Hon. William Pitt; Being an Impartial Vindication of the Conduct of the Ministry from the Commencement of the present war to this Time. In Answer to the Aspersions cast upon them by Admiral Byng and his Advocates* London, 1756.

   Attempts to discredit Pitt's efforts on behalf of Byng.

175. *The Resignation: Or, The Fox out of the Pit, and the Geese in, with B[yn]g at the Bottom* London, 1756.

   Strongly critical of Newcastle and Fox, advocates a public inquiry into the loss of Minorca and urges office for Pitt.

176. [Shebbeare, John]. *An Answer to a Pamphlet call'd The Conduct of the Ministry Impartially Examined. By the author of the Four Letters to the People of England* London, 1756.

   Anti-Newcastle and Fox.

177. Shebbeare, John. *An Appeal to the People: Part the Second* London, 1757.

   Bitterly critical of those in the city who had opposed mercy for Byng, praising Pitt for attempting to avert the admiral's execution.

178. Shebbeare, John. *A Fourth Letter to the People of England. On the Conduct of the Ministers in Alliances, Fleets and Armies since the*

first Differences on the Ohio to the taking of Minorca by the French
London, 1756. At least 6 editions.

Pro-Pitt. Amplifies the theme of ministerial culpability for the loss of
Minorca and appeals for a change of measures and men.

179. [Shebbeare, John]. *A Third Letter to the People of England. On
Liberty, Taxes And the Application of Public Money* London, 1756.

Urges strong colonial measures in line with Pitt's urgings in Parliament. Shebbeare was a well known ultra-Tory propagandist and occasional contributor to the *Monitor*, the essay paper founded by Richard
Beckford in 1755 to revitalize Toryism nationally and to further the cause
of Pitt. Shebbeare's arguments were refuted in *A Full and Particular
Answer to all the Calumnies, Misrepresentations and Falsehoods contained in a pamphlet called a Fourth Letter to the People of England*
London, 1756.

180. *A too hasty censure, February 15, 1757 and a too necessary retrac-
tion, March 20, 1757* London, 1757.

Attack on Pitt for his efforts to avert the execution of Admiral Byng.

THE MILITIA

181. *Further objections to the Establishment of a Constitutional Militia:
Being a reply to the Monitor* London, 1757.

182. *A Letter to the Right Honourable William Pitt Esq. wherein the
utility and necessity of a well regulated militia, during the French
War, is clearly demonstrated and all objections to it fairly stated
and fully confuted. By an Englishman* London, 1760.

183. *Proposals for Carrying on the War with Vigour, raising the supplies
within the year and forming a National Militia* London, 1757.

184. *Reflections on the Present State of Affairs: in which are introduced
some hints on the Militia Bill* London, 1756.

Copy in the Cambridge University Library, Ddd. 25.141. Author is
opposed to idea of a militia as proposed by Pitt.

185. [Shebbeare, John]. *A letter to the People of England, upon the
Militia, Continental Connections, Neutralities and Secret expeditions* London, 1757.

Supportive of Pitt's design for a national militia.

THE NEWCASTLE–PITT MINISTRY, 1757–1761

186. Cooper, John Gilbert. *The genius of Britain. An iambic ode. Addressed to the Right Honourable William Pitt* London, 1756.

187. [Dodington, George Bubb]. *The Honest Grief of a Tory expressed in a Genuine Letter from a Burgess of - - - - - - -, in Wiltshire, to the Author of The Monitor, February 17, 1759* London, 1759.

A viciously effective pamphlet designed to weaken the Tory-Pittite entente, by demonstrating the extent to which Pitt, in alliance with the Duke of Newcastle, had compromised traditional Tory principles.

188. [Douglas, John]. *Seasonable Hints from an Honest Man on the Present Important Crisis of a New Reign and a New Parliament* London, 1761.

Widely regarded as a Court Manifesto, the pamphlet, in outlining the anticipated advantages of George III's accession, clearly illustrates how the new reign would ultimately undermine Pitt's patriot credibility and reputation.

189. *The English Pericles, or, the four qualifications necessary to make a true statesman, exemplified in the character and conduct of Mr. Secretary Pitt* London, 1759.

Very eulogistic treatment.

190. *An Essay on Political Lying* London, 1757.

Attempts to discredit Pitt's claim to high office, belittle his nationwide popularity and promote the political interests of Henry Fox. The thrust of the pamphlet was reinforced by a sham reply *A Seasonable Reply to a Scurrilous Pamphlet called An Essay on Political Lying* London, 1757.

191. *The Father of the City of Eutopia, Or the Surest Road to Riches, dedicated to the Rt. Hon. Wm. Pitt, Esq.* London, 1757.

Copy at the Goldsmith's Library, University of London.

192. *For our country: An Ode, as presented to the Right Honourable William Pitt* London, 1757.

A laudatory poem.

193. [Jones, Henry]. *The patriot enterprize: or an address to Britain. A Poem, inscribed to the Right Honourable William Pitt* London and Dublin, 1758.

194. *A Letter from A Merchant of the City of London, to the Right Honourable William Pitt, Esq. Upon the affairs and Commerce of North America and the West Indies* . . . London, 1757.

Urges upon Pitt the vigorous pursuit of naval and colonial operations.

195. *A Letter to His Grace, the D[uke] of N[ewcastle]* London, 1757.

Urges a coalition between Pitt, his Tory supporters and the Duke of Newcastle.

196. *A Letter to the Right Honourable H[enry] F[ox]* London, 1757.

An attack on Pitt.

197. *An Ode, in Two Parts, Humbly Inscribed To The Right Honourable William Pitt* London, 1760.

Copy available at the Bodleian Library.

198. *Plain Reasons for removing a certain Gentleman by O. M. Haberdasher* London, 1759.

Comprehensive villification: accuses Pitt of being a demagogue, warmonger and opposed to peace as well as a Tory.

199. *Poetical epistle occasioned by the late change in the administration. Addressed to the Right Honourable William Pitt, Esq.* London, 1757.

A laudatory poem.

200. [Ruffhead, Owen]. *Ministerial Usurpation Displayed, and the Prerogatives of the Crown, with the Rights of Parliament and of the Privy Council, considered—In an Appeal to the People* London, 1760.

A criticism of ministerial despotism directed at the Pitt-Newcastle administration by a lawyer, turned pamphleteer, strongly confident in the abilities and reform aspirations of the new king.

201. *The Secret Expedition. A New Hugbug Ballad.* London, 1757.

Ballad muted in criticism of Pitt but concerned about his continental policy.

202. *The Speech of William the Fourth, to both Houses of P[arliament].* London, 1757.

A Broadsheet, maligning Pitt personally and politically in the crudest of terms.

203. *A Vindication of Mr. Pitt, By a Member of parliament* London, 1758.

Supportive of Pitt's domestic and foreign policy measures.

MILITARY EXPEDITIONS AGAINST FRANCE, 1757–1761

Much of the controversy surrounding the policy of amphibious operations was bound up with partisan politics. Because Pitt was a strong proponent of coastal expeditions, when these failed, political opponents and the press usually attempted to attribute failure to faulty planning and leadership on his part, rather than tactical problems, logistical factors or lack of initiative by the commanders involved.

204. *An Apology for W[illiam] P[itt] Esq. In Which the Conduct of L[ieutenant] G[eneral] B[ligh] is vindicated from all the Cavils thrown out against him* London, 1759.

A cutting satire both of Pitt and Bligh.

205. *An Appeal—Common Sense; or Striking Remarks on the conduct of L[ieutenant] G[eneral] Bl[i]gh and C[ommodo]re Lord [Howe] in the late Expedition on the Coast of France; wherein that unhappy affair is set in a more obvious light than has hitherto been* London, 1758.

Questions the military value of coastal expeditions and reflects adversely on Pitt's responsibility for such ventures.

206. *Candid Reflections on the Report (As Published by Authority) of the General officers* London, 1758.

Bitterly critical of Pitt, questioning the feasibility of expeditions per se and urging greater emphasis on British interests overseas. According to Walpole, the pamphlet may have been written by Dodington, one of Pitt's most inveterate political opponents.

207. *Considerations on the Proceedings of a General Court-Martial* London, 1758.

From the author of the *Candid Reflections* in reply to *The Expedition against Rochefort*. Crude anti-Pitt propaganda widely censured by contemporary reviewers.

208. [Dodington, George Bubb]. *An Examination of a Letter Published under the name of L[ieutenant] G[eneral] Bligh and addressed to the Hon. W. Pitt Esq.* London, 1758.

An abusive but clearly argued attack on Pitt for his altered stand on continental connections, the costly alliance with Prussia, his violation of the "true patriot" creed and alleged responsibility for the failed expedition to St. Malo.

209. *A Genuine Account of the Late Grand Expedition to the Coast of France* London, 1757.

Reaction to the public alarm over the failure of the Rochefort expedition. Raises doubts about the feasibility of the expedition, criticizes the performance of the commanders and stresses its inconsistency with Pitt's earlier pronouncements regarding continental measures.

210. *A Journal of the Campaign on the Coast of France* London, 1758.

An important source for the raid against St. Malo in June 1758. In addition to providing a full narrative of events, this pamphlet reprints much of the vital correspondence between Pitt and Admirals Anson, Howe and General Marlborough, the officers selected to command the expedition.

211. *A Journal of the landing of His Majesty's forces on the Island of Cape Breton and of the siege and surrender of Louisbourg: extracted from Major-General Amherst's and Admiral Boscawen's letters to the Right Honourable Mr. Pitt* London, 1758.

212. *A Letter from the Honourable L . . . t G . . . l B . . . gh to the Right Honourable W . . . m P . . . t Esq.* London, 1758.

One of 4 pamphlets produced in the aftermath of the failure of the St. Malo expedition in 1758. The author is critical of Pitt, the raid itself and Bligh's generalship. Argues that the administration should devote its attention to more worthwhile objectives in North America or the West Indies.

213. *The nature and utility of expeditions to the coast of France . . . with observations upon our late enterprises. By an officer in the late expedition* London, 1758.

Defends Pitt's handling of the St. Cast affair and views coastal expeditions as effective contributions to the war since these diverted the French from the war in Germany.

214. *An Ode on the expedition. Inscribed to the Hon. W . . . P . . . Esq.* London, 1757.

Verse rhyme. Supportive of coastal raids and Pitt's reliance on them.

215. [Perceval, John, Earl of Egmont]. *Things as they are* London, 1758.

Satirical attack on Pitt as the "initiator" of the "absurd and insignificant activity" of the coastal expeditions.

216. Potter, Thomas. *The Expedition against Rochefort Fully Stated and considered* London, 1758.

A reply to *Candid Reflections* by one of Pitt's political followers. Defends Pitt's planning ability and blames the military command for the Rochefort debacle.

217. *The Reply of the Country Gentleman to the Answer of his Military Arguments by the Officer* London, 1758.

Defends Pitt's scheme of coastal raids as the best use of Britain's limited forces. In such raids, a small expedition of men and ships striking anywhere could have the effect of a major field army through the element of surprise, forcing the French to protect their coasts at the expense of operations in Germany.

218. *A reply to the vindication of Mr. Pitt. By an English officer in the Prussian service* London, 1758.

A rebuttal of the previous pamphlet. Copies available in the Bodleian Library, Oxford.

219. *The Secret Expedition Impartially disclosed* London, 1758.

Argues that the Rochefort expedition miscarried because the commanders involved had been sent by Pitt on an impossible and badly planned assignment.

220. *The Secret Expedition. A New Hugbug ballad* London, 1757.

Although not overly hostile to Pitt, this pamphlet bitterly complains about the whole concept of amphibious raids and raises suggestions of possible Hanoverian influence on British policy.

221. *Things Set in A Proper Light. Being a full answer to a Noble Author's Misrepresentation of "Things As They Are"* London, 1758.

A disjointed and rather ineffectual reply to number 215.

222. *A vindication of Mr. Pitt. Wherein all the Aspersions thrown out against that Gentleman, relative to the Affair of Rochefort are unanswerably confuted. By a member of Parliament* London, 1758.

Defends Pitt by attributing failure of the Rochefort expedition to factional, political intrigues. Answers other criticisms of Pitt by highlighting the victories Britain was enjoying under his leadership and patriot appeal.

PEACE NEGOTIATIONS WITH FRANCE, 1759–1762

Of the very large number of pamphlets dealing with this subject, the following relate somewhat more particularly to Pitt.

223. *Considerations on the Importance of Canada and the Bay and River of St. Lawrence; And of the American Fisheries dependent on the Islands of Cape Breton, St. John's Newfoundland and the seas adjacent. Addressed to the Right Honourable William Pitt* London, 1759.

Urges a peace providing for the total expulsion of the French from North America.

224. [Douglas, John]. *A Letter Addressed to Two Great Men, On the Prospect of Peace; And on the Terms necessary to be insisted upon in the Negotiations* London, 1759.

Attributed by many contemporaries to Lord Bath, this pamphlet was almost certainly written by his protege and chaplain, John Douglas, probably with Bath's advice. Adopting a pro-Pitt line throughout, it supports the German war and urges the retention of Canada in any future peace.

225. Francis, Philip. *A Letter from the Cocoa-Tree To The Country Gentlemen* London, 1762.

Government manifesto, widely circulated and generally hostile to Pitt.

226. [Heathcote, George]. *A Letter to the Right Honourable The Lord Mayor, the Worshipful Aldermen and Common Council; The Merchants, Citizens and Inhabitants of the City of London. From an Old Servant* London, 1762.

Bitterly disparages the Bute ministry's secretive and conciliatory peace policy and urges a return to Pitt's firm stand against French duplicity and demands; only then would British victories be properly protected.

227. *A Letter to the People of England, On the Necessity of putting an Immediate End to the War, And the Means of obtaining an Advantageous Peace* London, 1760.

An appeal to Pitt for a moderate peace on the basis of lenient terms which France could accept.

228. *A Letter to the Right Honourable William Pitt Esq., On the Present Negotiations for a Peace with France and Spain* London, 1762.

Defense of Pitt's hard line policy towards France the previous year.

229. *Political Analysis of the War: The Principles of the present political Parties examined; And a just, national and perfect Coalition proposed between Two Great Men, whose Conduct is particularly considered* London, 1762. (Copy in the Widener Library, Harvard University)

A well written pamphlet urging the benefits of peace and recommending a coalition between Pitt and Bute to strengthen Britain's position in the negotiations.

230. *Reasons for Keeping Guadaloupe at a Peace, Preferable to Canada, Explained in Five Letters From a Gentleman in Guadaloupe to his Friends in London* London, 1761.

Representing important segments of City opinion, to which Pitt looked for support, this pamphlet urged the merits of Guadaloupe in contrast to Canada, as a permanent acquisition.

231. [Richardson, Edward]. *A Letter to a Gentleman in the City* London, 1762.

Richardson was one of Bute's pensioned writers. This pamphlet offers detailed arguments in favour of a moderate peace and is critical of Pitt's allegedly intransigent stand on peace the previous year.

232. [Ruffhead, Owen]. *Reasons Why the approaching Treaty of Peace should be debated in Parliament: As a Method most Expedient and Constitutional* London, 1760.

Stresses upon Pitt the Nation's need and desire for imminent peace.

THE GERMAN WAR

By 1760, public opinion in England was gradually but decisively turning against the German war, a development clearly reflected in the press where the issue revived the often bitter controversy, dating from Elizabethan days, over the interrelation between sea power and land operations, and over Britain's proper strategy in time of war. Waged intermittently until the signing of peace in 1763, this controversy produced a flurry of unusually cogent pamphlets, some supportive, more critical of continental intervention and the military expenditures this required. In most of these pamphlets, Pitt's liability or otherwise for Britain's current European involvement represented an important undercurrent to the main debate.

233. [Carlyle, Alexander]. *Plain Reasons for Removing a Certain Great Man from his M[ajesty's] Presence and Councils forever* London, 1759.

A widely noted and influential defense of Pitt's involvement in continental connections by the eminent Scottish divine. It uses Pitt's popularity, sustained by British victories overseas to obscure the issue of his responsibility for the country's European commitments.

234. *The Case of the British Troops serving in Germany* London, 1761.

Defense of Pitt's continental policy.

235. *A Consolatory Epistle to the Members of the Old Faction, occasioned by the Spanish war* London, 1762.

Argues that both Pitt and the Nation were deluded into a continental war by Newcastle and the "old Whigs". Also defends Pitt's resignation and acceptance of rewards.

236. *A Defense of the Letter from the Duchess of M . . . . gh in the Shades to the Great Man* London, 1759.

Traditional arguments against continental connections and bitter criticism of Pitt for his ambiguous and changing attitude towards Hanover and the German war. Claims that Pitt's popularity was based on public ignorance and his patriot professions insincere and inconsistent.

237. *A Fair and Compleat Answer to the Author of "The Occasional Thoughts on the Present German War"* London, 1761.

Rebuttal of Mauduit's criticism of Pitt and the German conflict.

238. [Francis, Philip]. *A Letter from the Anonymous Author of the Letters Versified to the Anonymous Writer of The Monitor* London, 1761.

Strong polemic against Pitt's German commitments building on the arguments originally advanced by Mauduit.

239. *A full and candid answer to a pamphlet entitled Considerations on the Present German War* London, 1760. Numerous editions.

Detailed rebuttal of Mauduit's critique. Defends Pitt's military policies as holding a crucial balance between Britain's overseas and vital European concerns. Justifies the Prussian alliance as a useful diversion of French resources from the colonial/maritime war.

240. *The Honest Grief of a Tory, Expressed in a Genuine Letter from a Burgess of [Calne] in Wiltshire, to the Author of the Monitor* London, 1759.

Anti-Hanoverian polemic, questioning Pitt's patriot reputation, his supposed achievements in office and his commitment to British interests overseas in view of Britain's deepening continental involvement.

241. *A Letter from the Duchess of M[a]r[lborough], In the Shades, To the Great Man* London, 1759.

Challenges Pitt's claims to patriotism and popularity by detailed references to inconsistencies in previous and current policies, especially those relating to subsidy treaties and commitments on the continent. Attacks Britain's involvement in the German war, particularly in alliance with Prussia and censures Pitt for his support of this involvement.

242. *A Letter from a Gentleman In the Country to His Friend in Town, On His perusal of a Pamphlet Addressed to Two Great Men* London, 1761.

Published in rebuttal to Douglas' work *A Letter Addressed to Two Great Men*. Arguments against the German conflict, Hanover and the Prussian alliance are along usual anti-continental lines.

243. [Massie, J.] *Observations relating to British and Spanish proceedings* London, 1762. Copy available in the Goldsmiths' Library, University of London, Senate House, Malet Street, London, WC1E 7HU

Attack on Pitt's continental strategy and alleged excessive subservience to West Indian interests.

244. Mauduit, Israel. *Considerations on the Present German War* London, 1760.

Compelling attack on the policy of continental intervention, promoted by Pitt, and the large army and army expenditures this required. Stimulated an avid press debate on British strategy, its proper aims and modalities, that continued beyond Pitt's resignation. Perhaps the most influential polemic on the subject to appear during the war years. Mauduit's subsequent pamphlets on the German War largely recapitulated the arguments set forth in the *Considerations*. The work went through 5 editions within a few months with a total printing of nearly 6000 copies, an extraordinary figure for an 18th. century pamphlet.

245. Mauduit, Israel. *Occasional Thoughts on the Present German War* London, 1761.

A lengthy and rather disjointed polemic against the continental war as prejudicial to the interests of Britain and Europe itself. Contrary to the *Considerations*, specific criticism of Pitt in this pamphlet is muted.

246. [Perceval, John, Earl of Egmont]. *Things As They Are* London, 1758.

A stinging and widely influential indictment of Pitt's continental programme by an accomplished pamphleteer and close adherent of the king.

247. [Perceval, John, Earl of Egmont]. *Things As They Are; Part the Second* London, 1761.

A lengthy, drawn out survey of the origins of the German War, bitterly hostile to continental connections, Prussia and to Pitt.

248. *The plain Reasoner or further Considerations on the Present German War* London, 1761.

Castigates operations in Germany for their wasteful expense and inconclusiveness but supports Pitt's alliance with Prussia as an originally well conceived response to the French threat to Hanover. Urges that Britain's involvement in Germany be ended without delay. Although the author professes to be Mauduit and the British Library Catalogue and the D.N.B. accept him at his word, the arguments deployed throughout the pamphlet do not support the attribution. (See also: *Monthly Review*, xxiv, (Jan. 1761), p. 87; *Critical Review*, xi, (Jan. 1761), pp. 760-77).

249. *A Political Analysis of the war* London, 1762.

Pro-Pitt.

250. *The Proper Object of the Present war with France and Spain considered and the independence of Great Britain vindicated from any connection with foreign politics* London, 1762.

Challenges Pitt's involvement in continental affairs and advocates the immediate abandonment of the German war and vigorous concentration on naval and colonial operations, especially in view of the newly declared war against Spain.

251. *Reasons in Support of the War in Germany in Answer to Considerations on the Present German War* London, 1761.

Argues that the German conflict is a greater drain on French rather than British military and financial resources and, therefore, has substantial diversionary value. Praises Pitt for developing a strategy which sucessfully kept France occupied in Europe while allowing Britain to take the offensive overseas.

252. *Remarks on Two Popular Pamphlets* London, 1760.

Strong defense of Pitt, Britain's European commitments and the Prussian alliance.

253. [Ruffhead, Owen]. *The Conduct of the Ministry Impartially Examined* London, 1760.

Defense of Pitt's continental strategy as an inevitable consequence of Austria's alliance with France and the need to protect Britain's European trade which French dominance on the continent could easily endanger.

254. *A Second Letter from Wiltshire to the Monitor on the Vindication of His Constitutional Principles* London, 1759.

Accuses both the *Monitor*, the pro-government paper, and Pitt of having abandoned their original principles with regard to continental measures. Condemns present British intervention in Germany as a futile and expensive distraction from the maritime/colonial war, for the extension of which Pitt was largely responsible.

255. *Things Set In a Proper Light* London, 1758.

A generally disjointed and feeble reply to *Things As They Are*. Wholeheartedly supportive of Pitt.

256. *A Vindication of the Conduct of the Present war in a Letter to* . . . . London, 1760.

Anti-Maudit and pro-Pitt, this piece defends the government's German policy as a vital distraction of French resources from the naval/colonial war. It argues that continental operations were not separate from but key parts of an integrated war plan. Also recalls the complex diplomatic considerations which had forced Pitt to adopt an interventionist policy.

PITT'S RESIGNATION AND PENSION

257. *An Address to the City of London* London, 1762. Copy in the Henry E. Huntington Library, San Marino, California.

Satirical attack.

258. Almon, John. *An Appendix to the Review of Mr. Pitt's Administration* London, 1763.

259. Almon, John. *A Review of Lord Bute's Administration* London, 1763.

Written with the assistance of Lord Temple, this lively pamphlet presents a grossly biased view of Bute's ministry but is almost ostentatious in its flattery of Pitt.

260. Almon, John. *A Review of Mr. Pitt's Administration* London, 1763.

A strong defense of Pitt's policies. Dedicated to Temple, the pamphlet, widely noticed and abstracted in other publications, ran through 5 editions and was translated into German and French.

261. *An Answer to the Letter from a Right Honourable Person to* . . . . . *in the City* London, 1761.

Accuses Pitt of resigning because of his inability to negotiate a generally satisfactory peace settlement with France. Denounces Pitt's pension as incompatible with his earlier stand on sinecures and rewards.

262. *An Answer to A letter to the Right Honourable The Earl of Bute in which the false Reasoning and absurd conclusions in that Pamphlet are fully detected and refuted* London, 1761.

A cogent defense of Pitt's pension and step-by-step rebuttal of the major accusations made against him in the pamphlet press.

263. *The Box Returned, Or the City Satisfied* London, 1761.

Hostile to Pitt's resignation and its circumstances.

264. *The Case of the late Resignation Set in a True Light* London, 1761.

Accuses Pitt of unconstitutional pretensions, of seeking despotism over his colleagues and the nation. Criticizes Britain's involvement on the Continent and argues that Pitt's reputation and achievements have been grossly exaggerated.

265. *A Certain great Man vindicated by a lover of his country* London, 1761.

Defense of Pitt's pension and resignation. This pamphlet prompted the city to proceed with its Address of Thanks to Pitt and urge the communities to do the same. Presents the viewpoint of Lord Temple's political faction.

266. *The Coalition: or an Historical Memorial of the Negotiations for Peace, between His High Mightiness of C[laremont] and His Sublime Excellency of H[ayes]* London, 1761.

Satire on both Pitt and Newcastle though more critical of Pitt, his alleged patriot pretensions, his Tory supporters and his putative arrogance and greed.

267. *The Conciliad or the Triumph of Patriotism. A Poem* London, 1761.

Satirical attack in verse.

268. *The Conduct of a Rt. Hon. Gentleman in resigning the Seals of his office justified by Facts, And upon the Principles of the British constitution* London, 1761.

A sophisticated defense of Pitt, covering his German policy, the constitutional propriety of his resignation and the moral-political viability of his pension. Makes the critical point that although having resigned, Pitt was still at liberty to offer his opinion and advice as freely as before. Stimulated a renewal of the pamphlet debate over Pitt's resignation following a brief lull.

269. *A Consolatory Epistle to the Members of the Old Faction; occasioned by the Spanish War* London, 1762.

Defense of Pitt.

270. *Constitutional Queries, Humbly Addressed to the Admirers of a Late Minister* London, 1761.

Criticism of Pitt's letter to the *Public Ledger* and of his reasons for resigning.

271. *An Earnest Address to the People of Great Britain and Ireland* London, 1761. Copy in the Bodleian Library, Oxford OX1 3BG

Supports Pitt's resignation as a justified protest against the Cabinet's refusal to heed his advice regarding Spain and defends the pension as a proper reward for past services. It also stresses Pitt's continued freedom to be active and advise in Parliament.

272. *The Equilibrium: Or, Balance of Opinions on a late Resignation. By a citizen of the World, Residing in London* London, 1761. Copy available in the Bodleian Library, Oxford OX1 3BG

Criticism of Pitt's Spanish policy, his precipitate resignation in time of need, but approval of the pension as being richly deserved.

273. *An Examination into the conduct of Mr. Pitt* London, 1761.

A pro-Pitt piece.

274. [Francis, Philip]. *A Letter from the Anonymous Author of the Letters Versified to the Anonymous writer of the Monitor* London, 1761.

A scathing assault on the *Monitor's* attempted defense of Pitt. "In this duel between the *Monitor* and Francis, the scurrilously personal tone of attack and defence came to a height and the whole resignation debate reached its climax." M. Peters, *Pitt and Popularity* (Oxford, 1980), p. 225.

275. [Francis, Philip]. *A Letter from A Right Honourable Person and the Answer to it, Translated into verse* London, 1761.

At least 5 editions by January 1762. The writer was a protege of both Henry Fox and Bute. This mocking versification and its sequel perhaps became the most noticed of all the attacks on Pitt. Imparting a personally hostile tone to the debate over Pitt's resignation and pension, this pamphlet also touched on major questions of constitutional significance—issues such as the relationship between King and minister and among ministers—which would reverberate through political discussions for the remainder of the decade.

276. *A Full Vindication of the Right Honourable Wm. Pitt and Wm. Beckford, Esqs. In Answer to A scurrilous Pamphlet, entitled, A Letter from a Right Honourable Person and the Answer to it, translated into Verse* London, 1761.

A weak attempt to neutralize the effect of Francis' annotated versification by providing an alternative version. There is a copy in the Goldsmiths' Library, Senate House, Malet Street, London, WC1E 7HU.

277. [Guthrie, William]. *A Letter to the Right Honourable The Earl of Bute, on a late important Resignation and its probable consequences* London, 1761.

At least 3 editions. Guthrie was a pro-government pamphleteer, here stressing the need for peace, national unity and disentanglement from the continent. He discounts any possibly negative impact of Pitt's resignation.

278. [Guthrie, William]. *A Second Letter to the Right Honourable the Earl of Bute by the Author of the First* London, 1761.

A strong criticism of Pitt's letter to Beckford of 17 October and strictures on the City's thanks and instructions. Interprets the pension as incompatible with the tenets of true patriotism and denies that Pitt had acceptable grounds for resignation.

279. *An Impartial Enquiry into the conduct of a late Minister* London, 1761.

Copies available in the Guildhall Library, London and the Wren Library, Trinity College, Cambridge. A sarcastic, fullscale attack charging Pitt with desertion of a nation in crisis, false patriotism, political opportunism and deviation from principle with regard to continental subsidies and alliances.

280. *Impartial Reflections upon the present State of Affairs With inciden-
tal Remarks upon certain recent Transactions In a Letter to a Friend*
London, 1761.

A comprehensive attack on Pitt's ministerial record, reasons for resigning and acceptance of a pension. Calls for an end to continental involvement and a return to true "British policies": exclusive concentration on the
naval/colonial war and destruction of French trade and shipping.

281. *The late administration epitomised; an epistle in verse to the Right
Honourable William Pitt* London, 1763.

282. *A Letter to His Grace the Duke of Newcastle. On the Present Crisis
in the Affairs of Great Britain. Containing Reflections on a late Great
Resignation* London, 1761.

Praises Pitt for the successes of the war but admits that the pension
compromised his reputation for disinterestedness and his patriot status.
Refers to Pitt as the Great Commoner.

283. *A Letter from A Patriot in Retirement, To the Right Honourable Mr.
William Pitt upon Resigning his Employment* London, 1761.

Praises Pitt's ministerial record and his achievements.

284. *A letter to the right honourable author of a letter to a citizen* London,
1761.

Satirical attack.

285. *A letter to the Right Honourable W . . . P . . . , By a citizen* London,
1761.

A reply to the letter of the elder Pitt to William Beckford, written to
explain his resignation. Includes text of Pitt's letter (pp. iii–iv) with
caption: A letter from a right honourable person to . . . in the city. Censures
Pitt as "an enemy to his King and country."

286. *The Patriot unmasked, Or A Word to his defenders* London, 1761.

A bitter attack on Pitt's Spanish policy, German commitments, acceptance of a pension, motives for resigning and allegedly bogus patriot
reputation. The pamphlet's central theme—that of false patriotism—is
clearly summarized in the ballad that closes the piece.

> Your Courtiers and *Patriots* 'mong other fine Things
> Will talk of their Country and Love to their Kings
> But their Mask will drop off if you if you shake but the Pelf
> And now show King and Country all centered Self.

287. *Philo-Patriae: A Certain Great Man Vindicated* London, 1761.

Standard defense of Pitt's policies, reasons for resigning and acceptance of pension.

288. *Reflections occasioned by the Resignation of a Certain Great Man. Particularly addressed to the Citizen of London* London, 1761.

Standard defense of Pitt's pension and resignation.

289. *Remarks upon a popular Letter. By a citizen of London* London, 1761.

Questions the moral and political propriety of the pension, the timing and motives of Pitt's resignation and develops the theme of false patriotism. Argues that Pitt's popularity was ill founded, based on mindless public adulation and dangerous, prompting him to aspire to the role of "leading minister".

290. *The Right Honourable Annuitant Vindicated. With a Word or Two in Favour of the other Great Man, in Case of his resignation* London, 1761.

A hostile response to Pitt's letter of 17 October in the *Public Ledger*, officially explaining the reasons for his resignation on 5 October and justifying his acceptance of a government pension. Maintains that Pitt resigned because of his inability to conclude a satisfactory peace with France and highlights the inconsistencies of his past career.

291. [Shebbeare, John]. *A Letter to the Right Honourable Author of a Letter to a Citizen* London, 1761.

An especially forceful attack surveying the whole of Pitt's career from 1757 to 1761. Stresses his inconsistencies in the German war, criticizes his bellicose policy towards Spain, his reasons for resigning and questions his status as a great war minister and reputation for political integrity.

292. *The tears of Old England for the loss of Mr. Pitt. Tune: The Children in the Wood* London, 1761.

A Ballad.

293. *The Unhappy Memorable Old Song, (As it is called) of the Hunting of Chevy Chase; Imitated in a Spick and Span New Ballad accommodated to the Present Times* London, 1761.

Reissued in 1762 with commentary on Newcastle's resignation.

294. *The voice of Britain: a poem on the late glorious dawn of ancient patriotism, and the later inglorious frustration by the dismission of the Right Honourable William Pitt Esq.* London, 1761.

Poetic tribute.

295. *A word to a Right Honourable Commoner* London, 1761.

Laments Pitt's resignation and acceptance of a pension. There is a copy in the Henry E. Huntington Library, San Marino, California.

WAR WITH SPAIN, 1762

296. *An Answer to the Observations on the Papers relative to the Rupture with Spain* London, 1762.

Critical of Pitt's Spanish negotiations (1760–1761) and reasons for resigning.

297. [Guthrie, William]. *A Third Letter to the Right Honourable The Earl of Bute: In Which the Causes and Consequences of the War between Great Britain and Spain are fully considered; And the Conduct of a certain Right Honourable Gentleman further examined* London, 1762.

A detailed and, for the most part, balanced evaluation of Pitt's measures on Spain, peace with France, Germany and the National Debt.

298. *Papers relative to the Rupture with Spain* London, 1762.

Official publication of the documents relating to the break with Spain designed to vindicate the Government's cautious policy towards Spain and rejection of Pitt's call for aggressive measures upon which the latter had based his resignation.

299. [Wilkes, John]. *Observations on the Papers Relative to the Rupture with Spain, Laid Before both Houses of Parliament . . . By his Majesty's Command. In a Letter from a member of Parliament, to a Friend in the Country* London, 1762.

Defense of Pitt's Spanish policy by the famous journalist and reformer. Criticizes the government sponsored publication of the official documents relating to the Spanish crisis, maintaining these had been selectively edited to justify administration and undermine Pitt's reputation.

PITT'S OPPOSITION TO THE STAMP ACT

300. *The Answer at Large to Mr. P . . . tt's Speech* London, 1766.

Critical reply to Pitt's famous speech favouring repeal of the Stamp Act.

301. *The Celebrated Speech of a Celebrated Commoner* London, 1766.

Pitt's speech against the Stamp Act, delivered on 14 January 1766.

302. Champigny, Bochart, Jean. *Supplement au Ministère de M. Pitt avec une recapitulation exacte de toutes les demarches de ce sage politique depuis le 5 Septembre 1761* Londres, 1766.

Various subsequent editions.

303. Dulany, Daniel. *Considerations on the propriety of imposing taxes in the British colonies for the purpose of raising a revenue by Act of Parliament* Annapolis, 1765.

A pamphlet which appears to have influenced Pitt's views on the American question. He mentioned it with approval several times and in his great speech of 14 January 1766 on the Stamp Act, reproduced many of its arguments, some verbatim.

304. *A Free and Candid Address to the Right Honourable William Pitt on the Present Posture of Affairs, both at Home and Abroad* London, 1765.

305. *Free and Candid Remarks on a late Celebrated Oration* London, 1766.

306. Hicks, William. *The nature and extent of parliamentary power considered in some remarks upon Mr. Pitt's speech in the House of Commons, previous to the repeal of the Stamp Act. With an introduction applicable to the present state of the colonies* New York, 1768.

307. *A Letter from a Gentleman in London to His Friend in the Country relating to the American Stamp Act, with Mr. P . . . t's and other speeches on the occasion* London, 1765.

308. *The Necessity of Repealing the American Stamp Act demonstrated* London, 1766.

Utilizes some of Pitt's arguments against the Stamp Act.

309. Pigott, Robert. *A Second letter from Mr. Pigott, near Geneva, to the Right Honourable William Pitt On the necessity and advantage of a taxation on the publick funds* London, 1767.

310. Plant, Thomas. *Joyful News for America and the downfall of the Stamp Act; now sing ye Britains, now the stamps is ore, for Pitt has been your friend and Bute's no more* Philadelphia, 1766.

311. *The Speech for Mr. P . . . and several others, in certain August Assembly on a Late important Debate* London, 1766.

PITT'S ACCEPTANCE OF AN EARLDOM, 1766

312. Almon, John. "The Congratulation, 1766" in: *An Asylum for Fugitive Pieces*, (London, 1766), vol. I , pp. 62–63.

A poetic tribute.

313. *Candid Answer to the Enquiry into the conduct of a late Commoner* London, 1766.

Pro-Chatham.

314. Cotes, Humphrey. *An Enquiry into the Conduct of a late Right Honourable Commoner* London, 1766.

Bitter criticism of Pitt's accession to the peerage; accuses him of collusion with Bute and the court.

315. *Dr. Williamson's Narrative of the Extraordinary case of a late Great Commoner* London, 1767.

This pamphlet suggests that Chatham might be going insane.

316. *E . . . l of Ch . . . m's Apology. A Poem* London, 1766.

In verse. Strongly anti-Chatham.

317. *An Epistle to the Right Honourable the Earl of Chatham* London, 1766.

A laudatory poem.

318. *An Essay on Patriotism, and on the Character and Conduct of some late famous Pretenders to that Virtue* London, 1768.

Satirical attack.

319. *A Free Appeal to the People of Great Britain on the Conduct of the Present Administration since the thirtieth of July, 1766* London, 1767.

Attacks the Chatham Ministry and Pitt's peerage.

320. *A genuine Collection of the several pieces of Political Intelligence Extraordinary, Epigrams, Poetry, etc. that have appeared before the Public in Detached Pieces* London, 1766.

A convenient collection of the press items attacking Chatham following his acceptance of a peerage in 1766. For full coverage, the pamphlet should be read in conjunction with *The New Foundling Hospital for Wit*, London, 1766.

321. *A letter from William, Earl of Bath, in the Shades, to William, Earl of Chatham at Court* London, 1766.

Questions political wisdom of accepting a peerage.

322. Lloyd, Charles. *An examination of the principles and boasted disinterestedness of a late Right Honourable gentleman. In a letter from an old man of business to a noble lord* London, 1766.

The "late Right Honourable gentleman" is Pitt; the "noble lord" is Lord North. The pamphlet is an attack on Pitt's popularity and supposed Patriot principles.

323. *An Ode to the Earl of Ch . . . m* London, 1767.

In verse. Anti-Chatham.

324. *A Short View of the Political Life of a Late R. T. Hon. Commoner* London, 1766.

This is an answer to *An Enquiry into the Conduct of the late Right Honourable Commoner.*

325. *The Trial of England's Cicero or the Four Important Articles of his being an Orator, a Patriot, an Author and a Briton* London, 1767.

Anti-Chatham: criticizes the peerage, Pitt's claim to patriotism and scathingly reviews his parliamentary speeches.

326. [Wilkes, John]. *A Letter to his Grace the Duke of Grafton* London, 1767.

Indicts Chatham for mock-patriotism and hypocrisy.

PITT'S LATER POLITICAL CAREER

327. *An authentic account of the part taken by the late Earl of Chatham in a transaction which passed in the beginning of the year 1778* London, 1778.

328. *Authentic memoirs of the Right Honourable the late Earl of Chatham* London, 1778.

329. Burke, Edmund. *Thoughts on the Cause of the Present Discontents* London, 1770.

A strongly partisan commentary upon political events, legitimating parties, organized opposition and the activities of the Chatham and Rockingham Whigs in denouncing the court system.

330. *Character of the Earl of Chatham* London, 1778.

Eulogy.

331. [Dalrymple, H.] *Rodondo, or The State Jugglers* Edinburgh, 1773.

An attack on Chatham and John Wilkes.

332. Davies, Thomas. *The characters of George the First, Queen Caroline, Sir Robert Walpole, Mr. Pulteney, Mr. Fox and Mr. Pitt reviewed* London, 1777.

333. Dawes, M. *A letter to Lord Chatham, on American affairs . . . with some thoughts on government* London, 1777.

334. Dawes, M. *A letter to Lord Chatham, concerning the Present war of Great Britain against America* London, 1776.

335. *A Letter to Sir William Meredith, in Answer to his late letter to the Earl of Chatham* London, 1774. At least 5 editions.

Upholds Chatham's objections to the Quebec Act.

336. Lucas, Henry. *A visit from the shades; or Earl of Chatham's adieu to his friend Lord Camden. To which is added an epitaphial inscription to the Memory of William Pitt, Earl of Chatham* London, 1778.

337. Meredith, William. *A Letter to the Earl of Chatham on the Quebec Bill* London, 1774.

Defends the Quebec Act against Chatham's strictures in the House of Lords.

338. *Plan offered by the Earl of Chatham to the House of Lords entitled "A Provisional Act for settling the troubles in America and for asserting the supreme legislative authority and superintending power of Great Britain over the colonies* London, 1775.

339. *The Political Conduct of the Earl of Chatham* London, 1769.

Admits Pitt's abilities but stresses his character flaws, inconsistencies, occasionally poor judgment and overweening ambition.

340. *Thoughts on the Late Transactions respecting the Falkland's Islands* London, 1771.

Widely read attack on Chatham's demand for strong measures against Spain.

341. *The upholsterer's letter to the Right Honourable William Pitt Esq. now Lord Chatham* London, 1768.

VII. Newspapers

Freed from government control after 1695, newspapers in London—whether daily, triweekly or weekly publications—had by Pitt's time become an important part of the capital's socio-political fabric, at once reflecting, shaping and coordinating public opinion on diverse matters of national concern.

Rapidly growing readership produced a concomitant proliferation of newspapers, all offering extensive coverage of foreign and domestic news, advertising, editorials and increasingly after 1770, lengthy reports of parliamentary proceedings. Many provincial papers also sprang up throughout this period, consisting almost entirely of extracts from the numerous London papers delivered outside the city by stage coach and postal services.

Since this expansion coincided with the growth of political contention in Hanoverian England, comment on politics was to provide a common denominator between the contents of all forms of newspaper, most at some point, willingly or reluctantly, adopting an identifiable political stance. Through the London press, opposition and pro-ministerial groupings established circuits of contact and communication linking all sectors of political society and placing the newspaper itself at the center of the political process. Hence the identification and analysis of specific content areas—such as the themes explored, materials deployed and arguments presented—can be a useful guide to the assumptions of those engaged in political debate as well as contemporary perceptions of politics and particular politicians. Certainly newspaper accounts of Pitt help to illustrate the nature, substance and influence of that popular reputation which contributed so substantially to his political appeal both in office and in opposition. At the same time, newspaper reports are not always correct: one cannot depend upon an isolated statement of fact but often needs to verify newspaper accounts by reference to other sources. For general surveys see:

342. Black, J. *The English Press in the Eighteenth Century* London, 1987.

343. Cranfield, George. *The Development of the Provincial Newspaper 1700–1760* Oxford, 1962.

344. Hanson, L. *Government and the Press, 1695–1763* Oxford, 1936.

345. Morison, S. *The English Newspaper* London, 1932.

346. Rea, R. *The English Press in Politics, 1760–1774* Lincoln, Neb., 1963.

Also essential is:

347. Crane, L. S. and Kaye, F. B. *A Census of British Newspapers and Periodicals 1620–1800* London, 1927. Revised 1966.

The most important newspapers, chiefly London based, featuring sustained political comment were:

348. *The Auditor.*

Pro-government weekly established in July 1762 under Arthur Murphy to support the *Briton.*

349. *The Briton.*

Pro-government weekly paper founded in 1762, with Tobias Smollett as editor, for the purpose of defending the Bute ministry's peace negotiations with France against the Pittite *Monitor.* Extracts are published in: John Wilkes ed. *Political Controversy*, 2 vols., (London, 1763).

350. *The Contest.*

A weekly paper founded to oppose the *Test.* Conducted by Owen Ruffhead from 23 November 1756 to 6 August 1757. Widely read, especially in the city, the *Contest* effectively defended Pitt and attacked the opposition by using anti-party, patriot rhetoric and arguments.

351. *The Gazetteer.*

London's oldest morning paper founded as a pro-ministerial publication in 1735. Influential and widely read in the city, it supported Pitt during the early years of his ministry but displayed growing hostility following his resignation in 1761, with polemical attacks that outweighed defenses of Pitt both in quality and quantity. The paper was taken over by *The Morning Post* in 1797. See: Robert L. Haig, *The Gazetteer: 1737–1797, a study in the Eighteenth Century English Newspaper* Carbondale, 1960.

352. *Lloyd's Evening Post.*

Triweekly paper founded in 1757, generally supportive of Pitt.

353. *London Chronicle.*

A thrice weekly evening paper established in January 1757. Supported Pitt at first but after the accession of George III, increasingly favoured the new Court. Proved generally hostile to Pitt throughout the resignation/pension debate and defended Bute in 1762/1763.

354. *London Evening Post.*

Triweekly founded in 1727. A leading purveyor of political and governmental information, the paper tended to be pro-Pitt, generally from December 1756 and even during the bitter controversy surrounding his resignation and pension in the fall of 1761.

355. *London Gazette.*

Official government newspaper established in 1665. Principal published source of foreign and home news and as such, widely extracted in other papers. Over time, the *Gazette*—editorially constrained by its government ties—became surpassed by privately owned papers and consequently declined in reputation and sales.

356. *The Monitor.*

Weekly paper set up under the patronage of Richard Beckford in 1755 to revitalize Toryism both nationally and in London and to defend the political interests and policies of Pitt. Published until 1765. On this publication see: Marie Peters, "The Monitor, 1755–1765: A Political Essay Paper and Popular London Opinion". (Ph.D. dissertation, University of Canterbury, New Zealand, 1974)

357. *Morning Chronicle.*

Daily London paper established in 1769.

358. *The North Briton.*

Pro-Pitt weekly opposition paper set up by John Wilkes in June 1762 to counteract the government funded *Briton.*

359. *Owen's Weekly Chronicle.*

Founded in April 1758, it was increasingly anti-Pitt after January 1760.

360. *The Public Advertiser.*

From 1744, the *General Advertiser*: changed to *The Public Advertiser* in 1752. Widely read daily paper, containing little political comment before 1762–1763; as a whole, tended to be politically non-partisan, publishing contributions both sympathetic and hostile to Pitt. Under its publisher, Henry Sampson Woodfall, the paper was involved in legal proceedings for printing reports of parliamentary debates and in 1774, the famous letters of "Junius". Complete files for *The Public Advertiser* exist only for the period 1768–1774.

361. *The Public Ledger.*

Founded in January 1760, edited by Griffith Jones, this daily paper rapidly rose to national prominence, especially among the commercial city readership for its advertising policy and trade as well as business news. Not strongly political to begin with, it was staunchly pro-Pitt by the time of his resignation in October 1761.

362. *St. James's Chronicle.*

Tri-weekly paper founded in April 1761. Carried substantial political commentary.

363. *The Test.*

Weekly paper, first issued on 6 November 1756 under the auspices of Henry Fox, with such contributors as Arthur Murphy and Dr. Philip Francis. Scurrilous in tone but generally well written, the paper aimed to discredit the Pitt-Devonshire administration by attacking its Tory affiliations and prominently linking Toryism with the Jacobite cause.

364. *The Universal Chronicle.*

Founded in 1757. Amalgamated with the Westminster Journal in 1760, after which it became strongly critical of Pitt.

VIII.   Journals and Periodicals

Like newspapers, journals and periodicals formed an integral part of the thriving Hanoverian publishing world. Widely distributed both in London and the provinces, these publications catered to an expanding reading public with what was becoming a popular type of journalism: eclectic in content, practical in presentation, rich in flexibility and variation. As instruments of mass communication, journals also came to play a vital political role, providing synoptic coverage of important issues, giving voice to various political positions and generally fostering controversy and polemic. Given the astonishing success of many 18th. century journals and magazines, we can regard the political articles they printed as reflecting the views of their readership and hence as indicators of public attitudes to particular issues and personalities in British political life.

365. *Annual Register*

An annual review of events of the preceding year founded by William Dodsley in 1758 and still published today. A fund of information on literature and politics, the *Annual Register* was generally noted for its balanced views and editorial impartiality, though it proved critical of Pitt following his resignation in 1761 and supportive of the Bute ministry's peace efforts.

366. *British Magazine*

Founded in 1759 by the publisher and bookseller John Newbery, with Tobias Smollett as editor and dedicated to William Pitt. Published in 1767, the *British Magazine* was renowned for its serialization of major works of fiction, fine essays on history, philosophy and aesthetics as well as incisive coverage of political events. Though opposed to the German War, it defended Pitt's other policies and stressed the necessity of a hardline peace with France.

367. *Court and City Magazine*

Periodical established in 1761 by Israel Pottinger and edited by the playwright Hugh Kelly until its discontinuation in 1765. Essentially a miscellany patterned on the *Gentleman's Magazine*. This publication contained essays on many diverse themes, including superior contributions to current political controversies and debates. Unlike most other magazines, it remained neutral during the bitter press war following Pitt's resignation, but displayed a dominant concern with trade, a close affiliation with London's mercantile groups and hostility towards the peace treaty concluded by Bute in 1763.

368. *Common Sense: or The Englishman's Journal*

Opposition political journal produced from 1737 to 1743. Supported by Lord Chesterfield and George Lyttleton, this periodical served as a forum for the "patriot" Whig opposition to Walpole led by Pitt in the Commons.

369. *Critical Review*

A Tory and Church publication founded in 1756 by Archibald Hamilton, an Edinburgh printer, in opposition to the *Monthly Review*. Published until 1817. Reflecting the range and combative style of its first editor, Tobias Smollett, the *Critical Review*—especially during its earlier years—featured articles from Samuel Johnson, David Hume and William Robertson. The journal's political orientation at first was pro-Pitt, but by late 1761, it was siding with Pitt's opponents.

370. *Gentleman's Magazine*

Influential periodical founded in 1731 by the London printer Edward Cave and published in altered formats until 1907. Often considered the first magazine, this journal always placed primary emphasis on providing entertaining reading but also furnished political news, printing accounts of parliamentary debates, extracts from leading newspapers and pamphlets and original articles, most of which supported Pitt until his resignation from office in 1761.

371. *Grand Magazine*

Published from 1758 to 1760. Editor unknown. Committed both in editorials and contributions to the Pitt administration. Especially vigorous in its praise of Pitt's aggressive peace policy towards France.

372. *Imperial Magazine*

A minor literary periodical running from January 1760 to July 1762. Noteworthy for the space it devoted to monthly surveys and analyses of events at home and abroad, the *Imperial* resolutely supported Pitt and London merchant interests in the peace negotiations with France.

373. *Literary Magazine*

Published from 1756 until 1758 with Samuel Johnson as its first editor. Under Johnson, the magazine was isolationist, strongly averse to Pitt's continental alliances and pursuit of the German War; however, after Johnson's departure in late 1756, editorial policy changed to staunch patriotism and a pro-war orientation.

374. *London Magazine*

Close rival and imitation of the *Gentleman's Magazine*, this journal was founded in 1732 and ran until 1785. Its consistent advocacy of the Pitt ministry during the years 1756–1761 did much to sway public opinion in Pitt's favour.

375. *Monthly Review*

Periodical established by Ralph Griffith in 1749. Published with various title changes until 1845. Influential and widely read, the *Monthly Review* supported Pitt during the early years of his administration, especially on the German War issue, but became increasingly critical following Pitt's resignation and acceptance of a pension.

376. *Scots Magazine*

Monthly journal founded in 1738 and published until 1817. Enjoying a wide readership, with heavy emphasis on political and historical topics, the *Scots Magazine* tended to impartiality, featuring essays both condemnatory and supportive of the Pitt-Newcastle coalition.

377. *Town and Country Magazine*

Published from 1769 to 1795. Archibald Hamilton was its first editor. It was generally written with distinction and includes some pieces sympathetic to the Chatham administration.

378. *Universal Magazine*

First appeared in 1747 and remained in print until 1815. Most of its contributors are anonymous though articles by Henry Fielding, Joseph Priestly and Lord Chesterfield have been identified. The journal included only limited political material but much of this defended and justified Pitt.

379. *Universal Visiter*

Published from January to December 1756. Designed to have a broad appeal, the journal also printed documents and articles urging Pitt's assumption of office following Newcastle's resignation in November 1756.

IX. Pitt's Life and Career

A. BIOGRAPHIES (*indicates especially useful works)

380. Adams, William. *English Party leaders and English parties from Walpole to Peel* London, 1878.

Contains a chapter on Pitt of no particular value.

381. Almon, John. *Anecdotes of the Life of the Right Honourable William Pitt, Earl of Chatham* 3 vols. London, 1793. (various editions)

Lightweight, highly laudatory in tone and frequently unreliable, this tribute by the eminent journalist and bookseller—a partisan of the Grenvilles—is useful for its account of parliamentary debates and the author's personal knowledge of Pitt's associates and contemporaries. Despite its biases, the work was to be extensively used by later biographers of Pitt. The first edition, published in 1792, appeared in 2 quarto volumes of 370 pages. The format of the second edition, published the same year, was changed to 4 volumes octavo while the third edition, brought out in 1793, appeared in the 3 volume octavo style adopted for subsequent printings. Other editions followed rapidly with the final seventh published in 1810.

382. *Ayling, Stanley. *The Elder Pitt: Earl of Chatham* London, 1976.

A plausible and impressive portrait but one that often delineates more than it explains. Excellent in gathering and vividly reconstructing the scattered traces of private life which Pitt attempted to keep secret. Makes extensive but critical use of the work of specialist historians.

383. Ayling, Stanley. "William Pitt, Earl of Chatham". An article in Herbert Van Thal ed. *The Prime Ministers* 2 vols. London, 1974–1975.

A 14 page introductory sketch based on secondary sources but readable and well informed.

384. Baker, George Fisher. "Pitt, William" article in *Dictionary of National Biography* vol. XV, London, 1921, pp. 1240–1253.

Refined in style, balanced treatment and well informed.

385. Brougham, Henry, Lord. *Historical Sketches of Statesmen who Flourished in the Time of George III* 2 vols. London, 1839.

Contains a sensitive, acute and balanced appraisal of Chatham's positive as well as less admirable qualities. In many ways, a remarkable work for its time.

386. Brown, Peter. *William Pitt, Earl of Chatham, The Great Commoner* London, 1978.

A pleasant, balanced and comprehensive biography which gives due prominence to Pitt's achievements without falling into the excessive and uncritical adulation of earlier authors. Based mainly on published sources, and occasionally inaccurate on minor points, the work is of greater interest to the general reader than academic specialists.

387. Earle, J. C. *English Premiers* 2 vols. London, 1871.

Has a few stories about Chatham but otherwise of little value.

388. Eyck, Erich. *Pitt versus Fox, Father and Son: 1735–1806* London, 1950. (original German version Zurich, 1946; reprinted by Octagon Books, New York, 1973)

Within the context of party development, the author reviews two generations of political rivalry between Henry Fox, William Pitt (Earl of Chatham) and their sons, Charles James Fox and William Pitt, the Younger. Somewhat popular in tone but providing suggestive insights into character and personality of the key protagonists.

389. Freemantle, A. "Britain's greatest war minister", *Contemporary Review*, CLXI (1942), pp. 163–167.

More eulogy than historical scholarship; of no special value. Obviously written against the background of World War Two.

390. Gibson, Edward. *Pitt: Some Chapters of His Life and Times* London, 1898.

Revealing on Chatham's last years and family life.

391. Godwin, William. *The history of the life of William Pitt, Earl of Chatham* London, 1783.

First full length biography by the dissenting minister and political reformer. Distinctly eulogistic: attributes Britain's decisive victory in the Seven Years War exclusively to Pitt's strategic mastery and supreme direction of the war effort. Is critical, however, of the Chatham administration.

392. Green, Walford. *William Pitt, Earl of Chatham and the growth and division of the British Empire, 1708–1778* New York, 1901.

Outdated and based on limited material but still pleasant to read, especially the coverage of Pitt's later life and career.

393. Harrison, Frederick. *Chatham* London, 1905.

Negligible.

394. Hearnshaw, F.J.C. *British Prime Ministers of the Eighteenth Century* London, 1928.

Contains a brief and valueless survey of Chatham's career, 1766–1768.

395. Jaspar, Marcel H. *William Pitt, Comte de Chatham, fondateur de l'Empire Britannique* Brussels, 1948.

Superficial and frequently inaccurate.

396. Long, John. *Mr. Pitt and America's birthright; a biography of William Pitt, the Earl of Chatham, 1708–1778.* New York, 1940.

Popular in tone and of no special value.

397. Macaulay, Thomas Babington. *The Earl of Chatham* New York, 1878. (Harper's half-hour series, vol. 38)

Candid, penetrating and written with absorbing skill.

398. Macaulay, Thomas Babington. "William Pitt, Earl of Chatham", *Edinburgh Review*, LVIII (1834), pp. 508–544. Various editions.

This famous essay—a review of Thackeray's *Life*—offers a characteristically elegant and insightful account of Pitt's career. The author recognizes the defects in Pitt's character and personality but also praises his accomplishments during the Seven Years War.

399. McDowall, A. S. *Life of Chatham* London, 1903.

A short sketch; valueless.

400. Mersey, Clive Bigham, 2nd. Viscount. *The Prime Ministers of Britain, 1721–1921* New York, 1924.

Chapter IV contains a 13 page balanced appraisal of Pitt's life and political career.

401. Müller, Karl Alexander von. *Der ältere Pitt* (Schriften der Corona) Munich, Berlin, 1937. 172 pp.

Translated by Eileen Taylor as *The Elder Pitt* New York, 1939. Designed for the educated general reader.

402. Pike, Royston. "William Pitt, Earl of Chatham", an article in Royston Pike ed. *Britain's Prime Ministers from Walpole to Wilson* London, 1968.

Charming vignette, depicting the private man behind the famous name.

403. Plumb, John Harold. "The Earl of Chatham", *History Today*, II, (1952), pp. 175–180.

A brief but instructive overview of Pitt's career by a stimulating author.

404. Plumb, John Harold. *Chatham* London, 1953. New edition in 1965.

A readable and popular presentation that attributes much, perhaps too much, to Pitt's mental instability. Particularly useful for its lucid portrayal of the political background.

405. Proebst, Hermann. *William Pitt, Begründer der Britischen Macht* Berlin, 1938.

Semi popular account of no special value.

406. Robertson, Charles. *Chatham and the British Empire* London, 1946. Reprinted in 1962, Collier Books edition and in 1984 by Greenwood Press.

Intended more as a study of the imperial issues with which Pitt was concerned rather than a standard biographical account, this book nevertheless contains much useful detail on his private life, health, political connections, etc. and throughout is sensitive to the interplay between personality and circumstance as determinative of much in Pitt's career.

407. *Rosebery, Archibald, 5th. Earl of. *Chatham, His Early Life and Connections* London, 1910.

A still valuable introduction to Pitt's life and career until 1756 by a stimulating and knowledgeable author. Marred by inadequate references to original sources.

408. Rosebery, Archibald, 5th. Earl of. *Pitt (English Statesman Series)* London, nd.

Of little value.

409. *Ruville, Albert von. *William Pitt, Earl of Chatham* 3 vols. London, 1907.

A translation of *William Pitt, Graf von Chatham* Stuttgart, 1905. Drawing on extensive manuscript sources, including the Prussian archives, this work is particularly illuminating on Pitt's handling of continental affairs and complex relationship with Frederick the Great. The author's often less than flattering remarks about the statesman's political opportunism constituted a conscious break with historiographic convention and gave rise to irate replies. (See: Harrison, F. "Address to the Fellows of the Royal Historical Society", *Transactions of the Royal Historical Society*, 3rd. Series, III (1909), pp. 34–39.

410. Salomon, Felix. *William Pitt der Jungere* Leipzig, 1901–1906.

Life of the younger Pitt but contains a suggestive chapter on Chatham.

411. Sherrard, O. A. *Lord Chatham: A War Minister in the Making* London, 1952.

Basically a work of hero worship, though useful for Pitt's early career. Weakened by its limited use of unpublished primary sources.

412. *Sherrard, O. A. *Lord Chatham: Pitt and the Seven Years War* London, 1955.

Gracefully written and provocative in judgment. Views the Newcastle-Pitt coalition as disastrous for Pitt's career and depicts Pitt as both creator and saviour of Britain's overseas empire. Tends to misunderstand the complex reality of 18th. century British politics and the factors shaping colonial policy at this time.

413. Sherrard, O. A. *Lord Chatham and America* London, 1958.

Covers Pitt's career from his resignation (1761) until his death. Sherrard seeks to absolve Pitt from sole responsibility for the political confusion of the early 1760's—a task in which he is only partially successful. He writes too much from Chatham's point of view and fails to consult some vital manuscript collections.

414. Taylor, George R. "The Pitt Family and its myths", *Modern English Statesmen* London, 1920. pp. 104–139.

Of no particular value.

415. *Thackeray, Francis. *A History of the Right Honourable William Pitt, Earl of Chatham* London, 1827. 2 vols.

Although sycophantic and uncritical in approach, this work is useful for its report of debates, copies of despatches and printed state papers dealing with the Seven Years War and, comprehensively, with the peace negotiations of 1760, conducted by Pitt. Essentially Thackeray's Pitt is a statesman but not a personality: he has no discernible human attributes or foibles.

416. Timbs, John. *Anecdote Biography: William Pitt, Earl of Chatham and Edmund Burke* London, 1860.

Numerous anecdotes collected from other works but not very critically edited.

417. Treasure, Geoffrey. "William Pitt, 1708–1778", an article in idem ed. *Who's Who in History London*, 1969. pp. 131–142.

A model of judicious compression.

418. *Tunstall, Brian. *William Pitt, Earl of Chatham* London, 1938.

A pleasantly written and stimulating study, based on extensive primary research, offering an interesting interpretation of Pitt's strategy and political views. Tends to re-enforce the views of Corbett and Williams.

419. Valentine, A. *The British Establishment, 1760–1784: An Eighteenth Century Biographical Dictionary* 2 vols. Norman, 1970.

Disappointingly brief entry.

420. *Williams, Basil. *The Life of William Pitt, Earl of Chatham* 2 vols. London, 1913. Reprinted by Octagon Books, New York, 1966.

Still the standard *Life* superseding all previous and subsequent biographies. Outstanding in detail and balance though outdated in its pre-Namierite treatment of eighteenth century British politics and somewhat weak on colonial policy. Tends sometimes to be uncritical in praise of Pitt's judgment and actions and unfair to his opponents'. Contains a valuable appendix listing Pitt's speeches according to date, subject and contemporary sources.

421. Williams, Basil. "William Pitt, Earl of Chatham (1708–1778)", an article in: Bonamy, Dobree ed. *From Anne to Victoria, Essays by various Hands* London, 1937. pp. 188–203.

Complimentary and generally unenlightening.

B. EARLY LIFE, FAMILY BACKGROUND AND GENEALOGY

Substantial information on Pitt's family background and early life can be found in all of the major biographical accounts listed above. To these should be added:

422. Austen-Leigh, R. A. *The Eton College Register* vol. 2. Eton, 1927.

423. Bruce, J. *Annals of the Honourable East India Company 1660–1778* 3 vols. London, 1810.

Useful for information on Pitt's grandfather, Governor Thomas or "Diamond Pitt".

424. Cokayne, George E. *Complete Peerage* 8 vols. London, 1887–1898.

425. Gibbs, Vicary. *The Complete Peerage* London, 1913. vol. III, pp. 144–145.

Provides basic biographical details.

426. Gilbert, D. *Parochial History of Cornwall* 4 vols. London, 1838.

Gives a good account of the Pitt family at Bocannoc, the Cornwall seat acquired by Governor Thomas Pitt.

427. Harwood, Thomas. *Alumni Etonenses* Birmingham, 1797.

428. Jesse, H. John. *Memoirs of Celebrated Etonians* London, 1875. Vol. II.

Helpful for Pitt's pre-political life.

429. Lever, Tresham, Sir. *The House of Pitt: A Family Chronicle* London, 1947.

Written in popular vein but contains significant material on the Pitt family as a whole and will guide the reader to a number of little known sources.

430. Mackenzie, T. M. *Dromana* Dublin, 1906.

Provides information on Pitt's maternal ancestors, the Fitzgeralds and the Villiers.

431. Maxwell Lyte, H. C. *A History of Eton College, 1440–1910* London, 1991.

Has useful information on Pitt's Eton days.

432. Yule, Henry, Sir ed. *Diary of William Hedges* (Hakluyt Society Publication) 3 vols. London, 1889.

Volume III contains a full account of the career of Pitt's grandfather with a revised pedigree of the Pitt family.

C. UNIVERSITY AND PARLIAMENT, 1726–1746

433. Chenevix French, Charles. *George II* London, 1973.

Helpful on Pitt's role as Paymaster in the Pelham administration.

434. Dragoon Guards. *Historical Records of the First or King's Regiment of Dragoon Guards* London, 1837.

Account of Pitt's regiment.

435. Foord, A. S. *His Majesty's Opposition, 1714–1830* Oxford, 1964.

Relates Pitt's political philosophy to his role in opposition, 1742–1744 and 1755–1757.

436. Foster, J. *Alumni Oxonienses, 1715–1886* London, 1887.

437. Hoare, R. C. *History of Wiltshire* 6 vols. London, 1822–1844.

Information about Pitt as MP for Old Sarum.

438. Ilchester, Earl of. *Henry Fox, First Lord Holland: His Family and Relations* 2 vols. London, 1920.

Good at demonstrating how Pitt's early opposition tactics hampered his political advancement.

439. Owen, John B. *The Rise of the Pelhams* London, 1957.

Contains interesting sections on Pitt's activities and tactics as opposition leader affiliated with Viscount Cobham, his connections with Frederick, Prince of Wales and the deliberations preceding his appointment to the office of Paymaster in 1746. Weak on the role of foreign affairs.

440. Owen, John B. "George II Reconsidered" in: *Statesmen, Scholars and Merchants: Essays in Eighteenth Century History presented to Dame Lucy Sutherland*, edited by Anne Whiteman, J. S. Bromley and P.G.M. Dickson, Oxford, 1973. pp. 114–134.

Utilizes the troubled relationship between George II and Pitt to illustrate that the king had more ability and was more of a force in politics than has generally been recognized.

441. Plumb, J. H. *Sir Robert Walpole* 2 vols. London, 1956, 1961.

Invaluable for Pitt's rise as an opposition spokesman.

442. Rosebery, Archibald, 5th. Earl of. *Chatham, His Early Life and Connections* London, 1910.

An interesting survey of Pitt's political career from his advent as MP for Old Sarum until the Devonshire-Pitt ministry, written by a man himself active in national affairs.

443. Sedgwick, Romney. *The History of Parliament, The House of Commons 1715–1754* 2 vols. London, 1970.

A vital source of political data and biographical information, prefaced by an important introductory essay. Volume II, pp. 355–356 deal with Pitt.

444. Wiggin, Lewis. *The Faction of Cousins: A Political Account of the Grenvilles* New Haven, 1958.

Although tending to be repetitious and didactic, Wiggin provides useful details of Pitt's rise in the political world, 1735–1756, against the background of his family connections with the powerful Grenvilles of Buckinghamshire.

445. Wilkes, John. *A Whig in Power: The Political Career of Henry Pelham* Evanston, Northwestern University Press, 1964.

In many ways an inadequate and misleading work, but one which provides a clear account of Pitt's tactics as opposition leader and the negotiations with Pelham leading to Pitt becoming Paymaster of the Forces.

D. PITT'S ESTABLISHMENT IN POWER AND POLITICAL STYLE, 1746–1761

446. Clark, J.C.D. *The Dynamics of Change: The Crisis of the 1750's and the English Party Systems* Cambridge, 1982.

A detailed narrative of high political manoeuvre from the general election of 1754 to the formation of the Newcastle-Pitt ministry in 1757. Curiously one dimensional, the work tends to overestimate Whig party solidarity and ideological consensus, but is insensitive to the importance of public opinion and extra-parliamentary political agitation in explaining Pitt's rise to power. Based on an impressive variety of sources and contains a valuable bibliography.

447. Colley, Linda. *In Defiance of Oligarchy: The Tory Party 1714–1760* Cambridge, 1982.

A book of admirable erudition, concerned primarily with the survival of a Tory party at the national and constituency levels after 1714, but also illuminating on the importance of Tory parliamentary support for Pitt's early political career.

448. Harris, George. *The Life of Lord Chancellor Hardwicke* 3 vols. London, 1847.

Of prime importance for every aspect of Pitt's political career until 1761.

449. Horn, D. B. "Diplomatic experience of Secretaries of State, 1660–1852", *History*, XLI (1956), pp. 88–89.

Makes the important but frequently forgotten point that Pitt had political strength but no diplomatic experience upon being appointed Secretary of State in 1756.

450. Hunt, William. "Pitt's retirement from office, 5 October 1761", *English Historical Review*, XXI (1906), pp. 119–132.

Illustrates the reasons for Pitt's resignation with documents from the Newcastle Papers in the British Library. See also the following supplements: Temperley, H.W.V. "Pitt's retirement from office", *English Historical Review*, XXI (1906), pp. 327–330; Schweizer, K. W. "The Cabinet Crisis of 1761: Unpublished Letters from the Bute and Bedford Manuscripts", *Bulletin of the Institute of Historical Research*, LIX (Nov. 1986), pp. 225–229.

451. Oldfield, T.H.B. *A History of the Boroughs of Great Britain* 3 vols. London, 1792.

Useful for Pitt's Seaford election, 1747.

452. Owen, J. B. "The Survival of Country Attitudes in the Eighteenth Century House of Commons" in: J. S. Bromley and E. H. Kossmann eds. *Britain and the Netherlands* vol. IV The Hague, 1971. pp. 42–69.

Suggestive on Pitt's relationship with the Tory MPs, 1754–1768.

453. Pares, Richard. *King George III and the Politicians* Oxford, 1953. New editions in 1954, 1959 and 1963.

Important post-Namierite analysis of the central direction of government during the reign of George III, containing perceptive reflections on Pitt's relations with the king, the Cabinet, opposition figures and party leaders placed within the context of key political events.

454. Rogers, Nicholas. "Resistance to Oligarchy: The City opposition to Walpole and his Successors, 1725–1747" in: John Stevenson ed. *London in the Age of Reform* Oxford, 1977. pp. 1–29.

Examines the forces which underlay the City's opposition to Walpole and his successors: an important dimension of Pitt's initial rise to political fame.

455. Sutherland, Lucy. "The City of London and the Devonshire–Pitt Administration, 1756–1757", *Proceedings of the British Academy*, XLVI (1960), pp. 147–173.

Perceptive study showing how Tory and metropolitan political support facilitated Pitt's entry into office following Newcastle's resignation in November 1756 and how the nature of this support, given Pitt's partisan reputation, imposed restrictions on his measures for domestic reform and recovery abroad. Given these restrictions, largely beyond Pitt's control, the author's estimate of the Pitt-Devonshire ministry as "confused and ineffective" seems overly harsh.

456. Sykes, N. "The Duke of Newcastle as Ecclesiastical Minister", *English Historical Review*, 57 (1942), pp. 59–89.

An authoritative account, pinpointing the role of ecclesiastical patronage in the political alliance between Pitt and Newcastle during the Seven Years War.

457. Thomson, Mark A. *The Secretaries of State, 1681–1782* Oxford, 1932. Reprinted by Frank Cass & Company, 1968.

Provides important details of Pitt's tenure as Secretary of State (South) in relation to the structure, organization and responsibilities of that office. Generally, the author, in common with other historians of the period, tends to exaggerate Pitt's control over foreign policy making and underestimate the influence of the Cabinet and the king, George II in particular.

458. Veitch, George. *The Genesis of Parliamentary Reform* London, 1913. Reprinted in 1965.

Sees Pitt as an important agent in the awakening of public interest in parliamentary affairs but basically conservative in his stand on political reform.

459. Wilkes, John. "British Politics Preceding the American Revolution", *Huntington Library Quarterly*, nr. 4 (1957), pp. 301–330.

Makes the important point that the Newcastle–Pitt coalition was successful as a war ministry but did little to solve the problem posed by domestic political instability and disorganization.

460. Yorke, Philip C. *Life and Correspondence of Philip Yorke, Earl of Hardwicke* 3 vols. Cambridge, 1913.

A monumental work, both a biography of Hardwicke and a compendium of papers from the rich Hardwicke collection in the British Library. Virtually every aspect of Pitt's public career in the 1740's and 1750's is touched upon.

E. THE CHATHAM MINISTRY, 1766–1768

461. Bateson, Mary ed. "A narrative of the changes in the ministry, 1765–1767", *Camden, New Series*, vol. LIX, London, 1898.

Prints many important letters from the Duke of Newcastle to his Nottinghamshire friend John White. (Originals in B.L. Add. MSS 33033) Although no longer privy to all that was happening at this time, Newcastle is nevertheless a revealing source for the circumstances preceding and accompanying the formation of the Chatham ministry.

462. Brooke, John. *The Chatham Administration, 1766–1768* New York, 1956.

A remarkably detailed and skilled account of a complex administration. The author effectively explains the motives of key figures in the milieu of London political manoeuvring and officialdom. Brooke concludes that Chatham's grandeur and aloofness "as well as his disastrous illness prevented a resolution of three critical problems: the American question, relations with the East India Company and the Wilkes affair". The work is also enlightening on Chatham's progressive alienation from the Rockinghamites and their corresponding drift into systematic opposition.

463. Brown, Lawrence. "The Grafton and North Cabinets, 1766–1775", University of Toronto Ph.D. dissertation, 1963.

Illuminating on the relationship between Chatham and Grafton and the implications of this for Cabinet politics and policy formation.

464. Brown, Peter. *The Chathamites: a study in the relationship between personalities and ideas in the second half of the eighteenth century* New York, 1967.

Attempts to demonstrate the influence of Pitt and Shelburne by examining the contributions of five of their followers whom the author calls "Chathamites": Dr. Richard Price, economist and prominent dissenter; Colonel Isaac Barré, soldier at Quebec and sympathetic to the American cause; John Dunning, barrister and MP; Bishop Jonathan Shipley, liberal cleric and friend of Benjamin Franklin; Sir William Jones, judge and philologist. An interesting attempt to illuminate politics by means of group biography.

465. Forster, Cornelius. *The Uncontrolled Chancellor: Charles Townshend and his American Policy* Providence, 1978.

Excellent on the personality conflicts behind the divisions within the Chatham ministry.

466. Johnson, E. "The Bedford Connection: The 4th. Duke of Bedford's Political Influence 1732–1771", Cambridge University Ph.D. dissertation, 1980.

Valuable for its analysis of Chatham's relations with the Bedford Whigs from 1766–1768.

467. Lawson, Philip. "Parliament and the First East India Inquiry, 1767", *Parliamentary History*, vol. 1 (1982), pp. 99–114.

Details the Chatham ministry's attempt to extract additional revenues from the East India Company within the context of Chatham's constitutional ideas on the Company's relations with the state.

468. Lawson, Philip. *The Imperial Challenge: Quebec and Britain in the Age of the American Revolution* London, 1989.

Has an excellent chapter on the Chatham ministry's Quebec policy showing that this policy was more constructive and determinative of subsequent developments than was traditionally believed.

469. Maccoby, S. *English Radicalism, 1762–1785* London, 1955.

Includes an incisive account of Chatham's ministry against the background of popular and opposition politics.

470. Merwin, Miles. "Lord Shelburne and America, 1760–1783", University of North Carolina Ph.D. thesis, 1971.

Interesting for its analysis of the interaction between Shelburne's and Chatham's personalities, the setting in which they operated and the importance of these factors for the shaping of colonial policy.

471. Middlekauf, Robert. *The Glorious Cause: The American Revolution, 1763–1789* New York, 1982.

Has short but perceptive section on the American policy of the Chatham ministry.

472. Namier, Lewis and Brooke, John. *Charles Townshend* London, 1964.

Authors argue that because of Chatham's illness at critical points, Townshend was able to take the lead in both East India politics and North American affairs—with disastrous results.

473. O'Gorman, Frank. *The Rise of Party in England: The Rockingham Whigs 1760–1782* London, 1975.

An outstanding study based on exhaustive research—particularly important for its coverage of Pitt's quixotic relationship with the major opposition groups, formation of the Chatham ministry and Chatham's later career, including his conciliation proposals for America.

474. Olm, Lee. "The Chatham ministry and the American colonies, 1766–1768", University of Michigan Ph.D. thesis, 1960. Contents are summarized in *Dissertation Abstracts*, vol. 21, (August, 19670), p. 334.

The scope of this thesis is less limited than the title might suggest, examining as it does the wider problem of imperial relations in the 1760's with special focus on the Chatham ministry's inability to relax Anglo-American tensions before these led to open hostility. Based on primary materials, including the Gage Papers and other manuscript collections at the William L. Clements Library in Ann Arbor, this work emphasizes the divergent concepts of Whiggism and the Glorious Revolution held by British and American political leaders—differences polarized by the confusions attending Rockingham's repeal of the Stamp Act, the timing of certain controversial British administrative decisions and the fact that these failed to provide essential colonial consensus. While acknowledging that the conduct of imperial relations was adversely affected by Chatham's prolonged illness, the author nevertheless concludes that even had Chatham retained his health, it is questionable whether he could have resolved the American problem given the incompatibility of British and colonial interests and convictions.

475. Ramsey, John F. *Anglo-French Relations, 1763–1770. A Study of Choiseul's Foreign Policy* Berkeley, 1939.

Shows in illuminating detail how French foreign policy after 1763 was shaped by the conviction that Pitt would renew the war between England

and France at the first favourable opportunity. Although Ramsey's central focus is always Choiseul, he does provide interesting reflections on the Chatham ministry's negotiations during the Manila and Falkland crises. Utilizes French and British archival materials.

476. Ritcheson, Charles. *British Politics and the American Revolution* Norman: University of Oklahoma Press, 1954.

Includes a fine chapter (III) analyzing the Chatham ministry's unsuccessful attempts to tackle the American problem in relation to Chatham's declining health, political factionalism, East Indian affairs and growing colonial recalcitrance.

477. Scott, Hamish. *British Foreign Policy in the Age of the American Revolution* Oxford, 1990.

Elegantly written and thoroughly researched, this work includes a brief but incisive account of Chatham's abortive attempts to secure a Northern League—based on core alliances with Russia and Prussia—as a counterweight to the Bourbon Courts. It further shows that Chatham's failure in the diplomatic sphere significantly impaired his ministry's stability and prospect of survival.

478. Sutherland, Lucy S. *The East India Company in Eighteenth Century Politics* Oxford, 1952.

Provides a classic account of the Chatham ministry's intervention in the East India Company's affairs. Argues that Chatham's attitude towards the company's policies was at all times highly ambiguous at best, a factor which combined with the fragmented nature of his administration and political configurations in parliament, helped shape the agreement finally reached between the government and the company in 1767.

479. Tracy, Nicholas. *Navies, Deterrence and American Independence: Britain and Seapower in the 1760's and 1770's* Vancouver, 1988.

Painstakingly researched but weak on the Chatham ministry's ineffective use of naval power as a diplomatic weapon, particularly over Dunkirk and in the case of the Manila ransom.

F. PERSONAL LIFE

480. Ashbourne, Lord. *Pitt: Some Chapters of his Life and Times* London, 1898.

Contains letters and other information about the Pitt children.

481. Climenson, E. J. *Elizabeth Montague* 2 vols. London, 1906.

Much information about Pitt's private life: his marriage, visits to Tunbridge Wells and relations with the Wests.

482. Howitt, W. *The Northern Heights of London* London, 1869.

Excellent description of Chatham's life at Hampstead.

483. Peach, R.E.M. *Life and Times of Ralph Allen of Prior Park* London, 1895.

Provides material on Pitt's visits to Bath and Prior Park.

484. Rose, J. Holland. *William Pitt and the National Revival* London, 1911.

Discusses Chatham's education of his children.

X.   Bibliographies

485. Andrews, C. M. *Guide to the materials for American History to 1783 in the Public Record Office* Washington, 1912.

486. Black, J. "British Foreign Policy in the 18th. Century: A Survey", *Journal of British Studies* vol. 26 (1987), pp. 26–53.

487. Christie, Ian. *British History since 1760: A Select Bibliography* London, 1970.

488. Davenport, F. G. "Materials for English Diplomatic History, 1509–1783", *Historical Manuscript Commission 18th. Report* London, 1917, pp. 357–402.

489. Elton, G. R. *Modern Historians on British History, 1485–1945* London, 1970.

490. Evans, Charles. *American Bibliography: A Chronological Diction-ary of all Books, Pamphlets and Periodical Publications . . . from 1639 to 1820* 13 vols. New York, 1941 (reprint edition)

491. Gephart, R. M. *Revolutionary America 1763–1789: A Bibliography* 2 vols. Washington, 1984.

492. Gipson, L. H. *A Bibliographical Guide to the History of the British Empire, 1748–1776* New York, 1964.

493. Grose, Clyde. *A Select Bibliography of British History, 1660–1760* Chicago, 1939.

494. Hecht, Jean. "The Reign of George III in recent historiography: a bibliographical essay", *New York City Public Library Bulletin* vol. 70 (May 1966), pp. 279–304.

495. *The Historical Association Guide to Historical Literature* New York, 1961.

496. Kellaway, William. *Bibliography of Historical Works issued in the United Kingdom, 1961–1965* London, 1967.

497. Kuehl, W. *Dissertations in History 1873–1960* University of Kentucky Press, 1965.

498. *National Union Catalogue. Pre 1956 imprints* vol. 460 London, 1976.

499. *National Union Catalogue: Supplement* vol. 750, London, 1981.

500. Pargellis, S. and Medley, D. J. *Bibliography of British History: The 18th. Century, 1714–1789* Oxford, 1951.

A supplement to this is currently being prepared by Professor Aubrey Newman of Leicester University.

501. Record, P. D. *A Survey of Thesis Literature in British Libraries* London, 1950.

502. The Royal Commission on Historical Manuscripts. *Guide to the Location of Collections Described in the Reports and Calendar Series 1870–1980* London, 1982.

503. *Royal Historical Society: Annual Bibliography of British and Irish History, 1975 to present.*

Various editors.

504. *Royal Historical Society: Writings on British History* London, 1934–1974.

Various editors.

XI. Contemporary Memoirs and Diaries Etc. Containing Important Material on Pitt

505. Albemarle, Lord ed. *Memoirs of the Marquis of Rockingham* 2 vols. London, 1852.

Although the editor's comments must be treated with caution, the volume contains important correspondence between the Whig leaders from 1760 onwards, including numerous letters from Pitt to Rockingham, now among the Wentworth-Woodhouse muniments in the Sheffield City Library. Informative on the policy of the Rockingham Whigs, their differences with Pitt and their efforts at reform.

506. Almon, John. *Anecdotes of the Life of the Right Honourable William Pitt, Earl of Chatham* 3 vols. London, 1973. Numerous editions.

A eulogistic work written by Almon to ingratiate himself with the younger Pitt who had recently sued him for libel. Contains accounts of debates drawn from contemporary sources but as a historical work, must be used with caution for the perspective throughout tends to be biased and uncritical.

507. Almon, John. *Memoirs of a Late Eminent Bookseller* London, 1970. Garland edition published in 1974.

Leading bookseller, publisher and pamphleteer: Almon had close contacts within Pitt's political circle. This volume contains correspondence between Almon and John Calcraft, political ally of Pitt after 1763, in which the latter is prominently mentioned. The originals of the letters are in the Perkins Library, Duke University, Durham, North Carolina.

508. Anson, William, Sir ed. *Autobiography and Political Correspondence of Augustus Henry, Third Duke of Grafton K.G.* London, 1898.

Invaluable for the Chatham ministry. Includes important correspondence with an excellent introduction but, being written from memory, is not always reliable for dates and facts and must be collated with other contemporary sources.

509. Bates, Albert ed. *The Fitch Papers* Hartford, 1918, vol. I.

Includes numerous communications between Pitt, as Secretary of State, and the colony of Connecticut concerning that colony's contributions to the campaign against French Canada, 1757–1758.

510. Bisset, A. ed. *Memoirs and Papers of Sir Andrew Mitchell* 2 vols. London, 1850.

Mitchell was Britain's envoy to Prussia from 1756 until 1764 and again from 1766 until his death in 1771. The *Memoirs* are based on portions of Mitchell's letters and dispatches located in the British Library (B.L. Add. MSS 58283–58367 and 6804–6872). Although this selection of papers throws valuable light on Pitt's relations with Frederick the Great and his continental policy generally during the Seven Years War, Bisset's edition is poorly edited and needs a modern replacement.

511. Brown, Peter and Schweizer, Karl eds. *The Devonshire Diary, 1759–1762* London, 1982.

Political Memorandum of William Cavendish, 4th. Duke of Devonshire, a widely respected statesman with an interesting independent view of affairs. Perhaps more than any other contemporary source, his diary illuminates Pitt's activities during the crises and developments of the years immediately preceding and following the accession of George III.

512. Butler, Charles. *Reminiscences* 2 vols. London, 1824.

Contains interesting reflections on Pitt by Charles Butler (1750–1836), a Roman Catholic barrister who was acquainted with the most distinguished men of his day.

513. Carswell, John and Drable, Lewis eds. *The Political Journal of George Bubb Dodington* Oxford, 1965.

A rich but sometimes suspect source covering the years 1749–1761. Especially useful for Pitt's relations with Leicester House, his role as Paymaster and subsequently as Secretary of State.

514. Channing, Edward and Collidge, A. C. eds. *The Barrington-Bernard Correspondence* London, 1912.

Occasional references to Pitt in letters from Lord Barrington to Governor Bernard (1761–1767). Negligible.

515. Coxe, William ed. *Memoirs of the life and administration of Sir Robert Walpole, Earl of Oxford* 3 vols. London, 1798.

Contains many useful documents, some relating to Pitt's early career.

516. Coxe, William. *Memoirs of the administration of the Right Honourable Henry Pelham* 2 vols. London, 1829.

Especially valuable for its reprint of letters (1743–1754) collected from various manuscript collections listed in the preface.

517. Creasy, E. S. *Memoirs of Eminent Etonians* London, 1850.

A few references to Pitt.

518. Fox, Henry. "Lord Holland's Memoir on the Events attending the death of George II and the Accession of George III", in: *The Life and Letters of Lady Sarah Lennox, 1745–1826*, edited by Countess of Ilchester and Lord Stavordale, London, 1901. Vol. I.

An interesting source for Pitt's final months in office by a jaundiced observer but one who had wit and understanding.

519. Glover, Richard. *Memoirs of a Celebrated Literary and Political Character* London, 1814.

Revealing account, especially for the period 1742–1757, by an admirer of Pitt.

520. Graves, R. *Recollections of the Late William Shenstone* London, 1788.

Describes Pitt's relations with the poet Shenstone.

521. Guttridge, G. H. ed. *The American Correspondence of a Bristol Merchant, 1766–1776* University of California Publications in History, 1934. vol. 22.

Has several references to Chatham's views on American taxation and his plan for colonial conciliation in 1775.

522. Hackmann, Kent. "George Grenville and English Politics in 1763", *Yale University Library Gazette*, 64 (April, 1990), pp. 158–166.

Prints two documents from the Yale University Library that illustrate the reasons for the failure of Pitt's return to office in the summer of 1763.

533. *Historical Manuscripts Commission Report. Manuscripts in various collections* (Eyre Matcham) London, 1909.

Important Dodington correspondence which throws light on Pitt's activities in opposition and as member of the Leicester House retinue.

524. Hodgart, M. ed. *Horace Walpole: Memoirs and Portraits* London, 1963.

Yields fascinating insights into Pitt's character and personality by an acute contemporary observer.

525. Jucker, Ninetta S. ed. *The Jenkinson Papers 1760–1766* London, 1949.

Numerous references to Pitt by an intelligent, well informed and often critical observer. Focuses frequently but far from exclusively on diplomatic concerns.

526. Labaree, L. W. ed. *The Papers of Benjamin Franklin* New Haven, 1959.

Volume 14 (January 1–December 1767) contains interesting observations on the foreign policy measures of the Chatham administration.

527. Lodge, Richard ed. *Private Correspondence of Chesterfield and Newcastle, 1744–1746* Camden 3rd. Series, vol. XLIV, London, 1930.

Important account based on the Newcastle papers of the political deliberations leading to Pitt becoming Paymaster of the Forces in 1746.

528. Lyttelton, George, Lord. *Works*, edited by Dr. Ayscough. London, 1775.

Poems and letters referring to Pitt.

529. McLelland, John ed. *The Letters of Sarah Osborn, 1721–1773* London, 1930.

Especially useful for the years 1766–1768.

530. Mure, William ed. *Selections from the Family Papers preserved at Caldwell. In Two Parts* Glasgow, 1854.

An interesting source for Pitt's connections with Bute, 1755–1760

531. Nichols, John. *Literary Anecdotes of the Eighteenth Century* 9 vols. London, 1812–1815.

Makes many references to Pitt.

532. Osborn, Emily ed. *Political and Social Letters of a Lady of the Eighteenth Century, 1721–1771* New York, 1891.

Contains observations on the Chatham administration by a humorously perceptive correspondent.

533. Oswald, James. *Memorials* Edinburgh, 1825.

A contemporary view of Pitt.

534. Phillimore, Robert ed. *Memoirs and Correspondence of George, Lord Lyttelton from 1734 to 1773* 2 vols. London, 1845.

Lyttelton, a friend and political supporter of Pitt, was a careful observer and his *Memoirs*, containing many references to Pitt, are particularly revealing for the period 1754–1763.

535. Redding, Cyrus. *Memoirs of William Beckford* 2 vols. London, 1859.

Provides interesting details about Pitt's later years.

536. Rose, George. *Diaries and Correspondence*, edited by L. V. Harcourt, 2 vols., London, 1859–1860.

Contains some confidential reflections by George III on Chatham.

537. Rose, George, Sir ed. *The Marchmont Papers* 3 vols. London, 1831.

Volume one is useful for Pitt's early political career, especially the period 1744–1746.

538. Russell, John, Lord ed. *Memorials and Correspondence of Charles James Fox* 3 vols. London, 1853.

Volume one (pp. 180–189) contains a firsthand account of William Eden's negotiations for Chatham's resumption of office in 1778.

539. Schweizer, Karl and Lawson, Philip eds. "A Political Diary by Charles Jenkinson, 13 May–29 June 1765", *Historical Research*, vol. 65 (October 1992), pp. 348–358.

Contains important material on Pitt's abortive negotiations for office in the summer of 1765 by a well informed and intelligent observer.

540. Sedgwick, Romney ed. *Letters from George III to Lord Bute, 1756–1766* London, 1939.

An invaluable source, authoritatively edited, for Pitt's declining relationship with Newcastle, Bute and the King, the originals of the letters being preserved at Mt. Stuart, Isle of Bute. This work, despite its excellent selections, is no longer complete since there are over 400 additional letters from George III to Bute, formerly in the Cardiff Public Library—now at Mt. Stuart, still not edited.

541. Seward, William. *Anecdotes of some Distinguished Persons* 4 vols. London, 1798.

Miscellaneous anecdotes about Chatham, mostly at second hand.

542. Smyth, H. W. *Aedes Hartwellianae, or Notices of the Mana and Mansion of Hartwell* London, 1864.

Contains Sir George Lee's "Memorandum of what passed between the Princess, Sir George, Mr. Pitt and Ld. Bute upon the coalition, 1755".

543. Tomlinson, John ed. *Additional Grenville Papers, 1763–1765* Manchester, 1962.

Contains important correspondence concerning Pitt's refusal to reenter the King's service in 1765 and the subsequent formation of the Rockingham administration.

544. Waldegrave, James, Earl. *Memoirs from 1754 to 1758* London, 1821.

Interesting estimate of Pitt's personality and character by a shrewd observer and frequent participant in public affairs. Gives the court version of the negotiations leading to the formation of the Newcastle–Pitt ministry in 1757. For a superior, modern edition, supplemented by Waldegrave's other unpublished writings and a lengthy introduction, consult: J.C.D. Clark. *The Memoirs and Speeches of James, 2nd. Earl Waldegrave, 1742–1763* New York, 1988.

545. Walpole, Horace. *Memoirs of the last ten years of the Reign of George the second*, edited by Henry Fox, 3rd. Earl Holland, 2 vols. 1822; 2nd. edition 3 vols., 1847.

Though Walpole's statements require verification in details, his general accuracy, especially for debates and political intrigues, makes him the leading contemporary recorder and vital source for the period 1751–1760. For Walpole's defects as a historian and chronicler see: J. W. Croker. "Walpole's Memoirs of the Reign of George II", XXVII (1822), pp. 178–215.

546. Walpole Horace. *Memoirs of the Reign of King George III* edited by G.F.R. Baker, 4 vols., London, 1894.

An illuminating diary by an astute, if often biased, observer with an interesting, independent view of affairs. Especially useful for the period 1760–1771.

547. Wheatley, Henry ed. *The Historical and Posthumous Memoirs of Sir Nathaniel William Wraxall, 1772–1784* 5 vols. London, 1884.

These memoirs actually cover the period up to 1789; lively, readable and generally unreliable.

548. Wyndham, Maud. *Chronicles of the Eighteenth Century* 2 vols. London, 1924.

An important account of the Lytteltons and their circle based on the manuscripts now at Hagley Hall, Stourbridge, Worcestershire. Especially valuable for Pitt's early career, the Pitt Family and the Grenvilles. Also contains quotes from the Dropmore Papers not published by the Historical Manuscript Commission.

549. Yorke, Philip C. *The Life and Correspondence of Philip Yorke, Earl of Hardwicke* 3 vols. Cambridge, 1913.

Incorporates extensive selections from the Newcastle and Hardwicke manuscripts. An important, carefully edited work, touching on virtually every phase of Pitt's career from his Leicester House days until 1767.

XII.   Special Topics

A. PITT AND THE SEVEN YEARS WAR, 1756–1761

i. Military/Naval Aspects

550. Barnett, C. *Britain and her Army, 1509–1970* London, 1970.

Chapter nine contains a valuable discussion of Pitt's military programme during the Seven Years War, viewed against the background of the historic national debate over Britain's proper strategy in time of war.

551. Baxter, Stephen. "The Conduct of the Seven Years War", chapter IX in Stephen Baxter ed. *England's Rise to Greatness, 1660–1763* London, 1983.

Substantiates other recent research, arguing that Pitt's overall political/administrative authority throughout the war was less extensive than such historians as Williams and Julian Corbett have claimed; makes the important point that the nature of 18th. century government—departmental, with ministers responsible only to the king—inevitably curtailed the ascendancy of any one man, however politically prominent.

552. Beaton, Robert. *Naval and Military Memoirs of Great Britain from 1727–1783* 6 vols. London, 1804.

Essentially a military chronology which ignores the political/administrative side of operations. Has little to say about Pitt's planning and strategy.

553. Beer, G. L. *British Colonial Policy 1754–1765* New York, 1933.

Contains useful discussion of Pitt's efforts to secure the service of colonial troops during the Seven Years War.

554. Black, Jeremy. "Naval Power and British Foreign Policy in the age of Pitt the Elder", in: J. Black and P. Woodfine eds. *The British Navy and the Use of Naval Power in the Eighteenth Century* Leicester, 1988, pp. 91–107.

Illuminating on the interaction of foreign policy and strategic questions which influenced Pitt's allocation of naval power during the Seven Years War.

555. Brewer, John. *The Sinews of Power: War, Money and the English State, 1688–1783* Cambridge, Mass., 1990.

Offers an enlightening discussion of how Pitt utilized Britain's military involvement in Europe during the Seven Years War to facilitate concurrent expansion of commercial and imperial interests.

556. Brown, J. W. "British Privateering during the Seven Years War, 1756–1763", Exeter University MA dissertation, 1978.

A good comprehensive study of its subject, offering interesting perspectives on Pitt's repeated attempts to profit by, but also control, privateering activity during the earlier years of the war.

557. Browning, Reed. *The Duke of Newcastle* New Haven/London, 1975.

A competent biography, offering a compressed but judicious account of the Newcastle-Pitt relationship and its impact on the formation of war policy during the Seven Years war.

558. Charteris, Evan. *William, Duke of Cumberland and The Seven Years War* London, 1925.

Old fashioned narrative but contains an interesting account of Frederick the Great's possible influence on Pitt's early strategy on the continent, 1756–1757.

559. Clayton, T. R. "The Duke of Newcastle, the Earl of Halifax and the American Origins of the Seven Years War", *The Historical Journal*, 24 (1981), pp. 571–603.

Counts Pitt among the "military men" led by Cumberland responsible for the formulation of an aggressive American policy in 1754 that made war with France virtually certain.

560. Corbett, Julian S. *England in the Seven Years War. A Study in Combined Strategy* 2 vols. London, 1907. Various subsequent editions.

A classic, if now dated, account of Britain's wartime strategy, especially enlightening on the relationship between Pitt's maritime and European operations. Argues that Pitt achieved victory by means of a military and naval strategy that was coordinated to the finest detail.

561. Entick, John. *The General History of the Late War* 5 vols. London, 1763–1764.

Comprehensive narrative of the war but remarkably muted, considering the date of publication, in its praise of Pitt.

562. Frazer, E. "The Pitt-Newcastle Coalition and the Conduct of the Seven Years War, 1757–1760", D.Phil. dissertation, Oxford, 1976.

An outstanding dissertation, providing a detailed analysis of the interaction between domestic politics and the formation of war policy from June 1757 until the death of George II in October 1760. In many ways superior to the work by Middleton.

563. Gipson, Lawrence H. *The British Empire: The Great War for Empire* vols. VI–VIII, New York, 1946–1953.

Carries a mildly old fashioned air, portraying Pitt as the consummate statesman and war leader. Excellent on the actual details of operations and campaigns and the administrative aspects of war making.

564. Gradish, Stephen F. *The Manning of the British Navy during the Seven Years War* London, 1980.

Significant work demonstrating how Pitt's solution of the Navy's manpower problem in 1758–1759 contributed to Britain's imperial success. Also argues convincingly that Pitt's effective distribution of naval resources was governed by a coherent strategic conception, enabling him to concentrate resources at the enemy's most vulnerable points.

565. Gradish, Stephen. "Wages and Manning: The Navy Act of 1758", *English Historical Review*, 93 (1978), pp. 46–67.

Presents William Pitt as co-sponsor (with George Grenville) of the Navy Act of 1758—legislation designed to strengthen the navy by solving the manning problem but which failed, owing to Parliament's unwillingness to provide the necessary funds.

566. Graham, Gerald S. *Empire of the North Atlantic: The Maritime Struggle for North America* Toronto, 1950.

Takes full account of the political, administrative and financial dimensions of the conflicts which propelled Britain to world power, but endorses the traditional view of Pitt as a heroic figure, whose inspired wartime leadership made success possible.

567. Hackmann, Kent. "The British Raid on Rochefort, 1757", *The Mariner's Mirror*, 64 (1978), pp. 263–275.

Examines Pitt's role in planning the Rochefort expedition and evaluates its longterm military effects.

568. Hackmann, Kent. "English Military Expeditions to the Coast of France, 1757–1761", University of Michigan Ph.D. dissertation, 1969.

Views the expeditions as integral parts of Britain's combined war effort and uses them to cast new light on Pitt's relationship with his fellow ministers as well as his military/naval commanders. A valuable study within its limits but needs to be strengthened by research in the French archives.

569. Hackmann, Kent. "William Pitt and the Generals: Three Case Studies in the Seven Years War", *Albion*, vol. 3, nr. 3 (1971), pp. 128–137.

Using the British expeditions to Rochefort, St. Malo and Cherbourg as case studies, Hackmann's piece shows that contrary to tradition, Pitt's role in the selection of commanders was minimal as was his contribution to the outcome of the operations—enemy strength, weather, terrain, troop morale and inter-service cooperation being the major factors promoting success or failure.

570. Holland-Rose, J. "A French Memoir on Pitt's naval operations of 1757–1758", *English Historical Review*, (1913), pp. 748–751.

Prints French criticism of English raids against Rochefort, St. Malo and Cherbourg from a document in the Chatham manuscripts.

571. Kennedy, Paul. *The Rise and Fall of British Naval Mastery* London, 1976.

Interesting and wide-ranging survey of Britain's rise to maritime pre-eminence. Credits the successes achieved during the Seven Years War to Pitt's inspired leadership and to the fact that he could perceive the war, both continental and overseas, as a strategic whole.

572. Lloyd, E. M. "The Raising of the Highland Regiments in 1757", *English Historical Review*, XVII (1902), pp. 466–469.

Establishes that the idea of raising Highland regiments for overseas duty did not originate with Pitt but praises him for actively promoting a measure which proved indispensable for waging successful war in North America.

573. Mackay, Ruddock. *Admiral Hawke* Oxford, 1965.

Provides some incisive observations on Pitt's belief in amphibious operations as a viable component of grand strategy during the Seven Years War.

574. Mahan, A. T. *The Influence of Sea Power upon History, 1660–1783* Boston, 1890. 1st. edition.

Widely read and often quoted classic, which argues that above all great power rivalries between 1660 and 1815 had their outcomes decided by maritime campaigns. Among other examples, Mahan uses Pitt's policies during the Seven Years War to illustrate this interpretation.

575. Manners, W. E. *Some Account of the Military, Political and Social Life of the Right Honourable John Manners, Marquis of Granby* London, 1899.

Deals in part with the reasons for Pitt's pursuit of the German War.

576. Mante, Thomas. *History of the Late War in North America* London, 1772.

Engrossed in the details of the war but virtually ignores Pitt's role.

577. Marcus, G. *Quiberon Bay: The Campaign in Home Waters, 1759* London, 1960.

Depicts Pitt as the driving force behind Britain's victories in the Seven Years War but recognizes Admiral Anson's administrative contributions to naval strength and efficiency.

578. McDermott, E. "The Elder Pitt and his Admirals and Generals", *Military Affairs*, 20 (1956), pp. 65–68.

Suggests that Pitt's achievements as war administrator have been exaggerated and calls for a reappraisal of Pitt's role in the conduct of the Seven Years War.

579. Middleton, Richard. *The Bells of Victory: The Pitt-Newcastle Ministry and the Conduct of the Seven Years War, 1757–1762* New York, 1985.

A revisionist study, written in limpid prose, which attributes Britain's stellar success during the Seven Years War more to the collective effort of the Pitt-Newcastle administration than solely to Pitt's leadership and strategic mastery as traditionally believed. Useful corrective to the inflated claims of earlier biographers but still fails to explain adequately the strength of Pitt's contemporary appeal. Also deplorably weak in its treatment of foreign policy issues.

580. Middleton, Richard. "British Naval Strategy 1755–1762. The West Squadron." *Mariner's Mirror*, 75 (1989), pp. 349–367.

A not altogether convincing attempt to show that Pitt played only a small role in Britain's naval successes during the Seven Years War.

581. Middleton, Richard. "Pitt, Anson and the Admiralty, 1765–1761", *History*, LV (1970), pp. 189–198.

A provocative essay which suggests that Pitt's wartime strategy was less novel than historians have traditionally assumed and his personal direction over military planning mitigated by administrative, financial and political constraints. Draws substantially on primary sources, both published and in manuscript.

582. Middleton, Richard. "A reinforcement for North America, summer 1757", *Institute of Historical Research Bulletin*, XLI (1968), pp. 58–72.

Documents Pitt's role against a background of administrative obstacles, in dispatching reinforcements to Lord Loudoun's army in July–September 1757.

583. Mullet, Charles F. "Military Intelligence on Forts and Indians in the Ohio Valley, 1756–1757", *William and Mary Quarterly*, vol. 3 (1946), pp. 398–410.

Prints intelligence report on French and Indian activities from Major John Smith, sent to Pitt by James Abercromby, colonial agent for South Carolina. Also includes Abercromby's observations on this report. The documents serve to illustrate Pitt's keen interest in Indian affairs and the problem of frontier defense. Original manuscripts are part of the Loudoun collection, Huntington Library, San Marino, California. (LO 4925, 4790)

584. Pares, Richard. *War and Trade in the West Indies, 1739–1763* Oxford, 1936.

Brilliant narrative, invaluable for Pitt's defense of West Indian interests throughout the Seven Years War. Also places West Indian campaigns within the economic/administrative context of Britain's imperial system.

585. Pargellis, Stanley. *Lord Loudoun in North America* New Haven, 1948.

Presents Pitt as a man of glaring contradictions, lapses and inconsistencies; moreover, tending to see issues in terms of logistics rather than strategy and exaggerating Pitt's administrative control, Pargellis unfairly attributes to Pitt predominant responsibility for the failure of the 1757 North American campaign.

586. Peckham, Howard. *The Colonial Wars, 1689–1762* Chicago, 1964.

Scholarly survey, containing useful information on Pitt's organization of the Louisbourg expedition in 1758. Tends to align with older works in seeing Pitt as solely controlling the main operations of the war.

587. Riker, T. W. "The Politics behind Braddock's expedition", *American Historical Review*, XII (1907–1908), pp. 742–752.

Useful for Pitt's involvement with the political faction, patronized by the Duke of Cumberland, which propelled the government to undertake the offensive in North America ending in Braddock's ill-fated expedition.

588. Rodger, N.A.M. *The Wooden World: An Anatomy of the Georgian Navy* Annapolis, 1986.

Offers interesting reflections on Pitt's naval strategy and the mechanisms for implementing that strategy.

589. Seeliger, Elizabeth. "Friedrich der Grosse und William Pitt", Leipzig University Ph.D. dissertation, 1942.

An excellent but little known study, making extensive use of Prussian archival material to examine in illustrative detail every facet of Pitt's association with Frederick the Great during the Seven Years War. Provides some interesting reflections on the military implications of the Anglo-Prussian alliance. Copy in the Cambridge University Library, microfilm 889.

590. Siebenick, Henry King. "William Pitt and John Forbes", *Western Pennsylvania Historical Magazine*, XXIV, nr. 2 (June 1941), pp. 69–92.

Concerns the re-naming of Fort Duquesne to Pittsburg in 1758.

591. Smelser, Marshall. *The Campaign for the Sugar Islands, 1759. A Study of Amphibious Warfare* Chapel Hill, 1955.

Discusses Pitt's role in planning for the amphibious operations against Guadaloupe and Martinique. Well researched but curiously one dimensional in failing to integrate these operations with Britain's other offensives during the Seven Years War.

592. Topley, D. N. "Privateering in the Seven Years War", Durham University MA dissertation, 1963.

Useful for Pitt's attempts both to encourage and control privateering activity during the period 1757–1761.

593. Western, J. R. *The English Militia in the Eighteenth Century* London, 1965.

Illustrates Pitt's political manoeuvres to secure the passing and enactment of the Militia Bill of 1758. Links the militia issue with the military imperatives of the Seven Years War by showing how Pitt exploited the invasion scare of 1759 and the need for British forces abroad to strengthen governmental arguments in favour of a militia.

594. Whitworth, Rex. *Field Marshal Lord Ligonier: A Story of the British Army, 1702–1770* Oxford, 1958.

Demonstrates in convincing detail Ligonier's influence on Pitt's planning of military and naval operations during the Seven Years War. The author is also among the first to question the traditional view of Pitt as solely instrumental in selecting and appointing commanders in the field.

ii. Diplomatic Aspects

595. Aiton, Arthur. "A neglected Intrigue of the Family Compact", *Hispanic American Review*, II (1931), pp. 387–393.

From evidence in the Spanish archives, he concludes that Pitt was accurate in his surmise regarding the seriousness of Spanish commitment to France in the summer of 1761 and hence justified in his demand for immediate hostilities against Spain.

596. Baugh, D. A. "Great Britain's blue-water policy, 1689–1815", *International History Review*, X (1988), pp. 33–58.

Provides important contexts to Pitt's strategic and diplomatic methods during the period 1756–1761.

597. Bourguet, Alfred. *Le Duc de Choiseul et l' alliance Espagnole* Paris, 1906.

Highly prejudiced interpretation of Pitt's negotiations with France and Spain in 1759–1761.

598. Bourguet, Alfred. "Le Duc de Choiseul et Angleterre: la mission de Monsieur de Bussy à Londres", *Revue Historique*, LXXI (1899), pp. 1–32.

Based on original documents but presents a grossly biased interpretation of events, blaming the failure of the negotiations wholly on Pitt and accepting French self-justifications at face value.

599. Carter, Alice. "The Dutch as neutrals in the Seven Years War", *International and Comparative Law Quarterly*, XII (1963), pp. 818–834.

Brief but detailed study, useful as an introduction to the developments preceding Pitt's Privateers' Act (1759) designed to reduce political tensions by restricting British depredations of Dutch and other neutral shipping.

600. Carter, Alice. *The Dutch Republic in Europe in the Seven Years War* London, 1971.

Deals in part with the genesis, enactment and results of Pitt's Privateers' Act of 1759. A sound, scholarly work based on British and Dutch manuscript sources.

601. Christelow, A. "Economic Background of the Anglo-Spanish War", *Journal of Modern History*, XVIII (1946), pp. 22–36.

Instructive on Pitt's unsuccessful attempts to prevent Anglo-Spanish differences from leading to all out war.

602. Conn, Stetson. *Gibraltar in British Diplomacy in the Eighteenth Century* New Haven, 1942.

Discusses Pitt's unsuccessful attempt in 1757 to secure a Spanish alliance against France by offering to restore Gibraltar, captured during the War of the Spanish Succession.

603. Doran, P. D. *Andrew Mitchell and Anglo-Prussian Diplomatic Relations During the Seven Years War* New York/London, 1986.

Originally a doctoral thesis, this work is helpful on Pitt's pragmatic policy towards Prussia but remains unrevised, hence outdated in various respects, and certainly fails to appreciate the complex factors governing the evolution and final collapse of the Anglo-Prussian alliance. See the review by K. W. Schweizer, "British Foreign Policy in the Eighteenth Century", *History of European Ideas*, 14 (1992), pp. 275–282.

604. Eldon, C. W. *England's Subsidy Policy towards the Continent during the Seven Years War* Philadelphia, 1938.

Detailed if somewhat ponderously written analysis of the policy of subsidizing European allies, giving special attention to the economic, military, strategic and domestic political pressures inducing Pitt to assume continental commitments upon his accession to office in 1756 and throughout the war. Remains the only monographic treatment of the subject.

605. Grant, William L. "Canada vs. Guadaloupe: An Episode in the Seven Years War", *American Historical Review*, XVII (July, 1912), pp. 734–743.

Traces influence of pamphlet literature concerning the Guadaloupe/ Canada controversy upon Pitt's mercantilist beliefs.

606. Grant, W. L. "La Mission de M. de Bussy à Londres en 1761", *Revue d'Histoire Diplomatique*, XX (1906), pp. 351–366.

Published separately as a pamphlet in Paris in 1906. Biased, superficial and unreliable account of Pitt's negotiations for peace during the summer of 1761 with the French delegate, François de Bussy.

607. Hall, Hubert. "Pitt and the Family Compact", *The Quarterly Review*, 190 (1899), pp. 333–355.

Utilizes a wide array of official and private records to assess the impact of the Family Compact as a major reason for Pitt's resignation in October 1761. Maintains that Pitt had positive knowledge of the existence of a Bourbon accord but does not explain convincingly how this was obtained.

608. Holland-Rose, J. "Frederick the Great and England, 1756–1763", *English Historical Review*, XXIX (1914), pp. 79–93 and 257–275.

One dimensional, thinly researched overview of Pitt's Prussian policy during the Seven Years War. Has been superceded in accuracy, points of detail and interpretation by Doran, Schlenke and Schweizer.

609. Hotblack, Kate. "The Peace of Paris", *Transactions of the Royal Historical Society*, II (1908), pp. 235–267.

An important work, based on archival research unfavourably comparing Lord Bute's peace negotiations with those of Pitt. Accepts and seeks to substantiate Pitt's verdict that the Peace of Paris was inadequate both as a return for conquests and a safeguard for British possessions overseas. While many of her strictures are justified, she ignores the fact that the treaty, despite its defects, did decisively establish Britain's maritime/colonial supremacy and mainly at the expense of France.

610. Hunt, W. "Pitt's Retirement from Office, 5 October 1761", *English Historical Review*, XXI (January 1906), pp. 119–131.

Uses extracts from the Newcastle Papers to illustrate the importance of the Anglo-French peace negotiations and growing hostilities with Spain in precipitating Pitt's resignation. See also Temperley, H.W.V. "Pitt's retirement from office, 5 October 1761", *English Historical Review*, XXI (1906), pp. 327–330. Supplements Hunt's work with documents from the Hardwicke Papers; Schweizer, Karl W. "The Cabinet Crisis of August 1761: Unpublished Letters from the Bute and Bedford Manuscripts", *Bulletin of the Institute of Historical Research*, LIX (November 1986), pp. 225–229. Amplifies the background to the cabinet crisis directly preceding Pitt's resignation with letters preserved among the Bute Papers, Mt. Stuart, Isle of Bute and the Bedford Papers, Woburn Abbey, Bedfordshire.

611. Hyam, Ronald. "Imperial interests and the Peace of Paris (1763)" in: Ronald Hyam and Ged Martin eds. *Reappraisals in British Imperial History* Toronto, 1975, pp. 21–43.

Provides balanced comparison between Pitt's terms of peace with those of the Bute administration. Concludes that Pitt's criticism of the peace agreement was largely wellfounded.

612. Lodge, Richard. *Great Britain and Prussia in the Eighteenth Century* Oxford, 1923. Reprinted by Octagon Books, 1972.

Includes a highly encomiastic and generally unbalanced account, chronologically as well as politically, of Pitt's relations with Prussia throughout the Seven Years War. Lodge is frequently incorrect about important details, utilizes only a narrow selection of British source materials and far over rates Pitt's commitment to the Prussian cause.

613. Pares, Richard. *Colonial Blockade and Neutral Rights, 1739–1763* Oxford, 1938.

Throws much light on Pitt's various attempts to control privateering excesses during the Seven Years War; also views these attempts against the background of neutral rights and the prize system as a whole.

614. Rashed, Z. *The Peace of Paris, 1763* Liverpool, 1951.

Uninspiring and, on the whole, poorly written—but does provide a full scale, if overly hostile, account of Pitt's negotiations with Bussy in 1761.

Stands badly in need of an up-to-date replacement both in scholarship and interpretation.

615. Reid, Marjorie. "Pitt's decision to keep Canada in 1761", *Canadian Historical Association, Reports* 1926. Ottawa, 1927. pp. 21–32.

Narrowly focused paper based on limited archival research; full of misleading generalizations, it makes the untenable claim that Pitt did not decide to keep Canada until the peace negotiations of 1761 and then only after a period of hesitation. More recent work has established that Pitt, an ultra-imperialist, was determined to retain Canada from the moment of its conquest in 1760.

616. Savelle, Max. *The Diplomatic History of the Canadian Boundary, 1749–1763* New Haven, 1940.

Chapter VII offers a sound analysis of Pitt's negotiations with the French envoy Bussy, March–September 1761.

617. Schlenke, Manfred. *England und das Friderizianische Preussen 1740–1763* Munich, 1963.

Analyzes the influence of public opinion, broadly interpreted, on Pitt's relations with Prussia during the Seven Years War. The standard work on the subject and an effective antidote to that narrow type of diplomatic history which views foreign policy as an isolated, self-contained activity unrelated to external forces and restraints.

618. Schweizer, Karl W. *Frederick the Great, William Pitt and Lord Bute: Anglo-Prussian relations, 1756–1763* New York, 1991.

Exhaustive study based on British, Prussian and other European archival sources. Particularly important for analyzing the political, fiscal and strategic pressures determining Pitt's fluctuating attitude towards the Anglo-Prussian alliance.

619. Schweizer, Karl W. "William Pitt, Lord Bute and the Peace Negotiations with France, May–September, 1761", *Albion*, XIII (Fall, 1981), pp. 262–275. Reprinted, slightly revised, in: Schweizer, Karl ed. *Lord Bute: Essays in Reinterpretation*, Leicester, 1988.

A corrective to French and British historiographical traditions: argues that Choiseul, not Pitt, was responsible for the failure to secure peace and demonstrates that Pitt wsa less intransigent and domineering in his handling of the negotiations than believed by scholars in the past. Makes extensive use of French, Prussian and British manuscript materials. See especially pp. 41–55.

620. Spencer, F. "The Anglo-Prussian Breach of 1762: An Historical Revision", *History*, (1956), pp. 100–112.

Portrays Pitt as less favourably disposed towards the Prussian wartime alliance than traditionally believed. An important work of historical reinterpretation.

B. PITT AND LORD BUTE

621. Almon, John. *History of the late Minority* London, 1766.

More political propaganda than serious history, though this hurridly written work was to have notable influence on Whig historiography in the nineteenth century. Strongly supportive of Pitt but excessively hostile to his opponents, especially the Earl of Bute.

622. Brewer, John. "The Faces of Lord Bute: A visual contribution to Anglo-American Political ideology", *Perspectives in American History*, VI (1972), pp. 95–116.

Provides fascinating account of how Reynold's portrait of Bute, completed in 1763, became a visual symbol of the sinister political role ascribed by so many contemporaries to Bute—a role in turn contrasted with the "patriot" virtues personified by Pitt.

623. Brooke, John. *King George III* London, 1972.

Highly critical of both Pitt and Bute, blaming both, in near equal measure, for the political instability of George III's early reign.

624. Elliot, G.F.S. *The Border Elliots and the Family of Minto* London, 1897.

A valuable source for Pitt's uneasy relationship with Bute especially after the accession of George III.

625. Lovat-Frazer, J. A. *John Stuart, 3rd. Earl of Bute* Cambridge, 1912.

Brief and old fashioned in its political analysis but offers balanced appraisals of the uneasy relationship between Bute and Pitt.

626. McKelvey, James L. *George III and Lord Bute: The Leicester House Years* Durham, North Carolina, 1973.

Surveys Pitt's relationship with Bute within the context of Leicester House politics, 1757–1760. Well researched but lacks literary imagination and flair.

627. Namier, Lewis. *England in the Age of the American Revolution* London, 1930. 2nd. edition, 1961.

Distinguished narrative and analysis of Pitt's relations with Bute and George III during the years 1759–1761 based on unrivalled knowledge of contemporary sources.

628. Newman, A. ed. "Leicester House Politics, 1750–1760, from the Papers of John, Second Earl of Egmont", *Camden Miscellany*, XXIII (1970), pp. 85–228.

Illustrates the weakening of Pitt's political position and deterioration of his relationship with Bute prior to and following the accession of George III.

629. Peters, Marie. "Pitt as a foil to Bute: the public debate over ministerial responsibility and the powers of the Crown" in: Schweizer, Karl ed. *Lord Bute: Essays in Reinterpretation* Leicester, 1988. pp. 99–115.

Enlightening exploration of how the public debate between supporters of Pitt and Bute generated rival constitutional theories about ministerial responsibility and the powers of the crown—questions that have ever since been central to discussions of George III's reign.

630. Ruville, Albert von. *William Pitt (Chatham) und Graf Bute* Berlin, 1895.

A perceptive analysis of the period 1760–1766 based on primary materials. Interesting is von Ruville's attempt, not altogether successful, to show how closely the political ideas of Pitt coincided with those of George III and Bute—the common source being the earlier programme of the 'Patriot' party. Generally the author here takes a more favourable view of Pitt than in his later biography. Some important European sources cited.

631. Schweizer, Karl W. "Lord Bute and the Press: the origins of the Press War of 1762 reconsidered" in: Schweizer, Karl ed. *Lord Bute: Essays in Reinterpretation* Leicester, 1988. pp. 83–98.

Extensively documented essay, arguing that Bute did not unleash a press attack on Pitt in 1761–1762 as historians have formerly maintained. It is established that so far from initiating the "Press War" of 1762, Bute became involved reluctantly and then only in defence against vilification directed at him by the Pittite press.

632. Schweizer, Karl W. "Lord Bute and William Pitt's resignation in 1761", *Canadian Journal of History*, vol. VIII, nr. 2 (September 1973), pp. 111–125.

Detailed study, based on archival material, showing that contrary to historical tradition, Bute did not scheme to ruin Pitt's reputation by offering him a pension following his resignation in October 1761.

633. Schweizer, Karl W. "William Pitt, Lord Bute and the Peace Negotiations with France, May–September 1761", *Albion*, XIII (Fall, 1981), pp. 262–275.

Makes the case that Bute rather than Pitt was the decisive force in the 1761 negotiations with France and that he devised a viable and coherent peace strategy.

634. Sedgwick, R. "William Pitt and Lord Bute: An Intrigue of 1755–1758", *History Today*, VI (1956), pp. 647–654.

Traces the inception and gradual deterioration of the political alliance between Pitt and Bute during the years 1755–1758.

C. PITT AND HANOVER

635. Black, Jeremy. "The Crown, Hanover and the Shift in British Foreign Policy in the 1760's" in: J. Black ed. *Knights Errant and the True Englishmen: English Foreign Policy 1600–1800* Edinburgh, 1989. pp. 113–134.

Excellent reappraisal of how George III's accession in 1760 influenced the attitude of Pitt and other politicians towards the Hanoverian connection. Modifies Dann's conclusions in important respects.

636. Dann, Uriel. "Hanover and Great Britain, 1740–1760", Oxford University, D.Phil. thesis, 1981. Published as *Hannover und England, 1740–1760: Diplomatie und Selbsterhaltung* Hildesheim, 1986.

Based on a wealth of manuscript material in British and continental archives, Dann's work offers an excellent account of the political difficulties which the Hanover issue presented for Pitt—forced to balance the often conflicting demands of George II, as elector, with those of his Hanoverian ministers. Tends to see the Anglo-Hanoverian relationship as harmful to Hanover, but fails to appreciate the frequently negative impact of Hanoverian policies on British concerns.

637. Doran, P. D. *Andrew Mitchell and Anglo-Prussian Diplomatic Relations During the Seven Years War* New York/London, 1986.

Published doctoral dissertation tracing Pitt's gradual abandonment of hostility to Hanover, once in office and showing how he exploited the initially popular Prussian alliance as a way of securing support for the electorate from an antagonistic House of Commons. Suffers from being unrevised and the author's failure to consult Hanoverian archival material.

638. Fuchs, Konrad. "England und Hannover in der Politik William Pitts des Älteren", *Niedersächsisches Jahrbuch für Landesgeschichte*, XL (1968), pp. 156–165.

Rather pedestrian treatment, based on secondary sources with special emphasis on Pitt's hostility to pro-Hanoverian policies during the War of the Austrian Succession. Tends to overestimate Pitt's executive preeminence and fails to recognize the extent to which Pitt was compelled by royal pressure to safeguard electoral interests during periods of crisis.

639. Mediger, W. "Great Britain, Hanover and the Rise of Prussia" in: *Studies in Diplomatic History. Essays in Memory of David Bayne Horn.* edited by R. Hatton and M. S. Anderson, London, 1970. pp. 199–233.

Provides the historical context for Pitt's decision to defend Hanover from French invasion after the outbreak of the Seven Years War. Makes extensive use of Hanoverian diplomatic papers.

640. Ward, Adolphus. *Great Britain and Hanover* Oxford, 1899.

Old fashioned diplomatic history based solely on British sources but still worthy of attention for its lucid summary of the factors which compelled British ministers, Pitt included, to safeguard Hanoverian security in times of war.

D. PITT'S VIEWS ON STRATEGY

641. Barnett, C. *Britain and her Army* London, 1970.

Shows that Pitt only gradually came to see the European and colonial conflicts as parts of a common, inter-related struggle, but that this realization helped him to formulate a successful global strategy.

642. Brown, Gerald S. "The Court Martial of Lord George Sackville, Whipping Boy of the Revolutionary War", *William and Mary Quarterly*, 9 (1952), pp. 317–337.

Documents Pitt's reorientation between 1757 and 1758 from a purely colonial/naval strategy to a wider war plan encompassing also military operations on the continent. Against this background, the author explains the reasons for Pitt's refusal to support Sackville following the latter's disgrace at the battle of Minden in 1759.

643. Pares, Richard. "American vs. Continental Warfare, 1739–1763", *English Historical Review*, LI (1936), pp. 429–465.

Indispensable for Pitt's position on the strategic controversy waged intermittently throughout the 18th. century over the interrelation between sea power and land war, between naval and military priorities and over the best policy to follow in light of national interests and resources. Also indispensable on this issue are the following:

The 4th. Earl of Sandwich: Diplomatic Correspondence 1763–1765 F. Spencer editor. Manchester, 1961. Note the introduction.

Baugh, D. A. "Great Britain's "blue-water" policy, 1689–1815", *International History Review*, X (1988), pp. 33–58.

644. Richmond, H. *Statesmen and Sea Power* Oxford, 1946.

An excellent introduction to Pitt's views on strategy and his continental policy during the Seven Years War.

645. Schweizer, Karl. "An unpublished Parliamentary Speech by the Elder Pitt, 9 December 1761", *Historical Research*, 64 (February, 1991), pp. 92–105.

Full formulation, in Pitt's own words, of the strategic principles underlying his military/naval policies.

646. Sosin, Jack. "Louisbourg and the Peace of Aix la Chapelle, 1748", *William and Mary Quarterly*, 14 (1957), pp. 516–535.

Of interest for Pitt's colonial/naval strategy during the War of the Austrian Succession. Shows that, when in opposition, Pitt favoured the abandonment of European campaigns and exclusive concentration on trans-maritime interests.

E. PITT AS A PARLIAMENTARY ORATOR

647. Butler, Charles. *Reminiscences* 2 vols. London, 1824–1827.

Good accounts of Chatham's oratory.

648. Butler, Henry Montague. *Lord Chatham as an Orator* Oxford, 1912.

Praises Chatham as an orator of genius, who improvised in the course of debate rather than delivering set speeches. Butler illustrates this through an analysis of Chatham's speeches in the House of Lords from January 1770 to 7 April 1778.

649. Grattan, Henry. *Memoirs of the Life* London, 1839.

Offers vivid glimpses of Pitt's oratorical style.

650. Rea, Robert. "Anglo-American parliamentary reporting: a case study in historical bibliography", *Bibliographical Society of America, Papers* XLIX (1955), pp. 212–229.

Draws together and analyzes the varying accounts of Chatham's speech to the House of Lords on 20 January 1775, following his offer to withdraw the British troops under General Gage from Boston.

651. Schweizer, Karl W. "The Speeches of William Pitt, 1st. Earl of Chatham: A note on sources", *Canadian Journal of History*, XXVII (April 1992), pp. 185–190.

A supplement and update of B. Williams' list of sources for Pitt's speeches (1736–1778).

652. Stephen, Leslie. "Chatham, Francis and Junius", *English Historical Review*, III (1888), pp. 233–249.

Discusses the connection of Sir Philip Francis and "Junius" with reports of Chatham's speeches in 1770 and presents the possibility that Francis was "Junius".

653. Turberville, Arthur. *The House of Lords in the 18th. Century* Oxford, 1927. Reprinted by Greenwood Press, 1970.

The standard survey, dated but still useful for its judicious coverage of Chatham's performance in the House of Lords, 1766 to 1778.

654. Williams, Basil. *The Life of William Pitt, Earl of Chatham* 2 vols. London, 1913. Reprinted by Octagon Books, New York, 1966.

Volume two has an appendix evaluating the major sources for Pitt's speeches.

F. PITT, PUBLIC OPINION AND THE PRESS

655. Brewer, John. *Party Ideology and Popular Politics at the Accession of George III* Cambridge, 1976.

Contributes an interesting outline of the nature and consequences of Pitt's popular reputation, especially in the 1760's as reflected in the press.

656. Bullion, John. "The *Monitor* and the Beer Tax Controversy: A Study in constraints on London Newspapers, 1760–1761" in: K. W. Schweizer and J. Black eds. *Politics and the Press in Hanoverian Britain* Lewiston, New York, 1989. pp. 89–117.

Analyzes the reasons for the *Monitor's* unexpected if temporary break with Pitt in 1760–1761 over the Beer Tax issue.

657. Gee, Austin. "English provincial newspapers and the politics of the Seven Years War, 1756–1763", University of Canterbury MA dissertation, 1985.

Excellent study of Pitt's evolving reputation as reflected in the provincial press.

658. Knapp, Lewis. "Smollett and the elder Pitt", *M.L.N.*, LIX (1944), pp. 250–257.

Surveys Smollett's judgment of Pitt over a period of 25 years and concludes that this judgment, expressed in diverse publications, was both impartial and significant.

659. Knight, C. L. "A Certain Great Commoner: the political image of William Pitt, first Earl of Chatham in the Colonial Press", *Proceedings of the American Philosophical Society*, 123, nr. 2 (April 1979), pp. 114–123.

660. Langford, Paul. "William Pitt and Public Opinion, 1757", *English Historical Review*, LXXXVIII, (1973), pp. 54–80.

Demonstrates that the agitation in favour of Pitt in the summer of 1757 was Tory inspired. These tributes, argues Langford convincingly, were designed to confirm Pitt's patriot status, promote his re-entry into office and impose some control on his future conduct.

661. Nobbe, George. *The North Briton: A Study in Political Propaganda* New York, 1939.

Documents Pitt's opposition to press controversy. Also illuminating on Pitt's disapproval of Wilkes.

662. Peters, Marie. "The *Monitor* on the Constitution, 1755–1765: new light on the ideological origins of English radicalism", *English Historical Review*, LXXXVI (1971), pp. 714–729.

Traces in part, the importance of Pitt's career, as reflected in the London press, for the evolution of mid-18th. century popular radicalism.

663. Peters, Marie. "The *Monitor*, 1755–1765: A Political Essay Paper and Popular London Opinion", University of Canterbury Ph.D. thesis, 1974.

A firstrate study, which uses the *Monitor*, the political essay paper founded by Richard Beckford in 1755, to illustrate the close relationship between Pitt's political career, the press and the growth of London radicalism.

664. Peters, Marie. *Pitt and Popularity: The Patriot Minister and London Opinion during the Seven Years War* Oxford, 1980.

A scholarly, well written monograph, showing how important Pitt's popular base and patriot reputation were between 1756 and 1761 and how the political press was used both to defend and challenge these assets throughout the Seven Years War.

665. Rea, Robert. "The Earl of Chatham and the London Press, 1755", *Journalism Quarterly*, 31 (1954), pp. 186–192.

Author shows that William Pitt's failure to appreciate and utilize the power of the Press provides important insights into the relationship between publishers and politicians on the eve of the American Revolution.

666. Rea, Robert. *The English Press in Politics, 1760–1774* Lincoln, Nebraska, 1963.

Now standard narrative on the topic, containing a fine chapter on the importance of the London press for Pitt's political career, especially following the accession of George III.

667. Rogers, Deborah. *Bookseller as Rogue: John Almon and the Politics of Eighteenth Century Publishing* New York, 1986.

First biographical study, based on original sources, of an important writer, bookseller and publisher. Deals in some detail with Almon's various publications about or on behalf of Pitt.

668. Rogers, Nicholas. *Whigs and Cities: Popular Politics in the Age of Walpole and Pitt* Oxford, 1989.

Highly readable and exhaustively researched study of urban politics in the early Hanoverian period. Especially useful for its analysis of Pitt's rise to power within the context of London urban agitation on his behalf. More thoroughly than previous accounts, it traces the interaction of press influence, economic interest, political clientage and ideological factors in this process. Revised and expanded version of the author's earlier work: "London politics from Walpole to Pitt: patriotism and independency in an era of commercial capitalism, 1738–1763". University of Toronto Ph.D. thesis, 1975.

669. Rude, George. *Wilkes and Liberty: a social study of 1763 to 1774* Oxford, 1962.

A distinguished study which sees the political uncertainty following Pitt's resignation and the prominence of Bute as key factors in the widespread discontent enhancing Wilkes' appeal among the lower classes, especially in the metropolitan area.

670. Spector, Robert. *English Literary Periodicals and The Climate of Opinion During The Seven Years War* The Hague, 1966.

Excellent coverage of the periodical literature on Pitt, 1755 to 1761.

G. PITT AND THE ROCKINGHAM WHIGS, 1762–1766

671. Brewer, John. "Rockingham, Burke and Whig Political Argument", *Historical Journal*, 1 (1975), pp. 188–201.

Shows how Pitt's political identity after 1761, resting largely on his precarious patriot status, depended upon joining neither party-minded Whigs nor Court politicians.

672. Collyer, C. "The Rockingham Connection and Country Opinion in the Early Years of George III", *Proceedings of the Leeds Philosophical and Literary Society*, vii (1952–1955), pp. 251–275.

A straight narrative of political events; little on Pitt.

673. Guttridge, G. H. *The Early Career of Lord Rockingham, 1730–1765* Berkeley, 1952.

Concerned primarily with Rockingham, but also shows clearly how much the success of a united Whig opposition, after 1762, depended on Pitt.

674. Hardy, A. "The Duke of Newcastle and his Friends in Opposition, 1762–1765", Manchester University MA dissertation, 1956.

Provides a still useful analysis of the factors behind Pitt's failure to concert policy with the mainstream Whigs.

675. Hoffman, Ross J. *The Marquis: A Study of Lord Rockingham 1730–1782* New York, 1973.

Perceptively analyzes the relationship between Rockingham and Pitt against the key political events of the period. Sees Pitt as the critical factor in the dissolution of the Rockingham administration.

676. Imlach, G. M. "Earl Temple and the Ministry of 1765", *English Historical Review*, XXX (1915), pp. 317–321.

Sees the possible revival of Cumberland's influence as a major reason for Temple's refusal to form a ministry with Pitt in May and June 1765.

677. Jarrett, D. "The Regency Crisis of 1765", *English Historical Review*, LXXXV (1970), pp. 282–316.

Discusses George III's regency bill of 1765 in the context of the King's attempt to persuade Pitt and the Whig opposition to cooperate with the Bute-Cumberland alliance for the purpose of ousting the Grenville ministry. Also explains why Pitt declined to form an administration under these circumstances; he was opposed to the Bill and the Court intrigues that produced it and he trusted neither Bute nor Cumberland.

678. Kemp, Betty. *Sir Francis Dashwood: An 18th. Century Independent* New York, 1967.

Helpful for Pitt's opposition tactics after 1761.

679. Langford, Paul. *The First Rockingham Administration, 1765–1766* Oxford, 1973.

Well written, meticulously documented narrative and analysis of Pitt's failure to cooperate with the Rockingham opposition in the years after 1762. Still the only full length study of its subject; valuable supplement to O'Gorman's work.

680. O'Gorman, Frank. *The Rise of Party in England: The Rockingham Whigs 1760–1782* London, 1975.

Shows Rockingham and followers to have been more divided in their attitude towards Pitt than is apparent from Langford's account. Provides the best analysis extant of the Rockingham ministry's prolonged yet futile attempts to obtain the cooperation of Pitt.

681. Sutherland, Lucy. "Edmund Burke and the First Rockingham Ministry", *English Historical Review*, XLVII (1932), pp. 46–72.

Helpful on the implications of Pitt's erratic behaviour between 1763 and 1766 for the Rockingham Whigs's attempts to secure London based commercial support.

682. Watson, D. H. "The Duke of Newcastle, the Marquis of Rockingham and the Mercantile Interests in London and the Provinces 1761–1768", Sheffield University Ph.D. dissertation, 1968.

Soundly researched, comprehensive account of Pitt's fluctuating relationship with Newcastle and Rockingham Whigs against the background of mercantile influence and opinion. Especially useful on Pitt's continuing popularity in the capital and the implications of this for successive ministries.

683. Winstanley, D. A. *Personal and Party Government* Cambridge, 1910.

A narrative of the struggle for political supremacy between George III and the opposition Whigs from 1760 to the downfall of the first Rockingham ministry. Winstanley attributes the King's success to Pitt's misguided refusal to support the Whig party in 1766, thereby making possible a royal authority that led eventually to constitutional abuses and disaster in America. In general, it reflects outmoded assumptions, but is still not entirely superseded by the works of O'Gorman, Brooke and Langford, even though the latter present much new manuscript material.

H. CHATHAM AND THE ROCKINGHAM OPPOSITION, 1769–1773

684. Elofson, W. M. "The Rockingham Whigs in Transition: the East India Company issue 1772–1773", *English Historical Review*, 104 (1989), pp. 947–974.

Demonstrates in detail how the Rockinghams' performance in the East India Company issue damaged their political relations with Chatham's opposition followers.

685. Fitzmaurice, Edmund, Lord. *Life of William, Earl of Shelburne, with extracts from his papers and correspondence* 3 vols. London, 1815. Revised edition in 2 volumes, London, 1912.

Based chiefly on the Lansdowne manuscripts and useful for Pitt's relations with the Rockingham faction.

686. Guttridge, G. H. "The Whig opposition in England during the American Revolution", *Journal of Modern History* VI (1934), pp. 1–13.

Traces the impact upon Britain's American policy of the relations between the Rockingham Whigs and Chatham and his supporters. Sees Chatham as more sympathetic towards America than seems justified in the light of current research.

687. Hoffman, Ross J. *The Marquis: A Study of Lord Rockingham 1730–1783* New York, 1973.

Excellent in its coverage of the Middlesex remonstrance, showing that Chatham's connections with metropolitan politicians and the popular cause they represented, rendered impossible any enduring cooperation with the Rockingham leadership.

688. O'Gorman, Frank. *Edmund Burke: His Political Philosophy* London, 1973.

Useful in demonstrating how the Rockingham party's reliance on extraparliamentary forces and city interests widened the rift with the Chathamite group.

689. O'Gorman, Frank. *The Rise of Party in England: The Rockingham Whigs 1760–1782* London, 1975.

Shows in convincing detail how North's prudent handling of the Falkland Islands crisis prevented Chatham and the Rockingham Whigs from mounting an effective opposition strategy.

690. Olson, Alisa Gilbert. *The Radical Duke: Career and Correspondence of Charles Lennox, third Duke of Richmond* Oxford, 1961.

Offers interesting sidelights and illustrative correspondence on Chatham's limited impact in opposition politics (1769–1772). Shows that the apex of Rockingham-Chatham collaboration had been reached by 1770 and explains the disputed issues over which relations deteriorated from then on.

691. Winstanley, D. A. *Lord Chatham and the Whig Opposition* Cambridge, 1912. Reprinted by F. Cass, 1966.

Pre-Namierian in outlook, hence tends to exaggerate the eclipse of Monarchical authority under George I and II; however, based on original sources and still essential for its insights on Chatham's alienation from and final break with the Rockingham connection. Believes that George III acted to strengthen royal authority and was ultimately successful because Whig factions led by Chatham, Rockingham and Grenville lacked the unity and failed to master the political skills necessary for victory.

I. PITT AND COLONIAL AFFAIRS

Inevitably, Pitt features to some extent in virtually every work on colonial history or imperial policy during the period 1748–1776. Hence, monographs are only listed if they are of direct interest and have a particular contribution to make.

692. Atkins, Walsh P. G. "Shelburne and America 1763–1783", Oxford University D.Phil. dissertation, 1971.

A careful work of research, interesting and revealing in its treatment of the Chatham-Shelburne relationship against the background of Anglo-American politics.

693. Bargar, B. D. *Lord Dartmouth and the American Revolution* Columbia, South Carolina, 1965.

Chapter XIV provides a convincing interpretation of Chatham's conciliation proposal (1775) as a propaganda tactic—to raise public opinion against the North ministry—rather than a serious piece of colonial legislation.

694. Basye, A. H. *The Lords Commissioners of Trade and Plantations* New Haven, 1925.

Traces Pitt's opposition to the creation of a secretaryship for the colonies and resistance to attempts by the Board of Trade to increase its powers in colonial affairs.

695. Brown, W. A. *Empire or Independence; A Study in the failure of reconciliation, 1744–1783* London, 1941.

Argues, on the whole convincingly, that Chatham's efforts for conciliation on behalf of the American colonies helped to make the war unpopular and hence, increased the government's difficulties. The work also shows clearly that Chatham's plan would not have been accepted in America: it left unresolved too many grievances and its rejection by the Lords saved the Americans from great embarrassment.

696. Chaffin, Robert. "The Townshend Acts of 1767", *William and Mary Quarterly* 3rd. series, xxvii (1970), pp. 99–102.

Provides strong arguments that the actions of Grafton and Townshend from 1766 require a revision of traditional interpretations of the Chatham ministry's policy towards America—viz that this policy was not as liberal as formerly believed and hence, failed to stem the rising tide of American dissent.

697. Christie, I. R. "The Earl of Chatham and American Taxation, 1774–1775", *The Eighteenth Century*, 20 (1979), pp. 71–83.

Clarifies some important but common misconceptions about Chatham's views on American taxation.

698. Christie, Ian and Labaree, Benjamin. *Empire or Independence 1760–1776* New York, 1976.

Includes a clear and intelligent account of Pitt and the Stamp Act, the authors arguing that Pitt's tactics preceding and during the parliamentary campaign for repeal were both designed to promote the disintegration of the Rockingham ministry and prepare for his return to office. Also valuable in showing how Chatham's illness in 1766 exacerbated Cabinet disagreements over colonial issues, caused critical delays in needed decisions and ultimately had serious repercussions on Great Britain's American policy.

699. Cone, Carl. *Burke and the Nature of Politics: The Age of the American Revolution* Lexington, 1957. vol. I.

Deals with Pitt in passing: suggestive on his relationship with Burke, the reasons behind his opposition to the Stamp Act and the formulation of his plan for the conciliation of America.

700. Coupland, R. *The American Revolution and the British Empire* New York, 1965. Reprint of 1930 edition.

A good introduction to Pitt's views on imperial governance and trade relations.

701. Donoughue, Bernard. *British Politics and the American Revolution: the path to war, 1773–1775* New York, 1964.

Analyzes in detail, with much new material, how the conflicting personalities of Chatham and Rockingham and their differences over colonial policy in 1774–1775 hampered the effectiveness of their respective followers in opposing the American measures of the North administration.

702. Douglas, David ed. *English Historical Documents: Volume IX: American Colonial Documents to 1776* London, 1955.

Contains a section (pp. 699–726) on the Pitt-Grafton Ministry and the Colonies, 1767–1768, together with illustrative documents. Emphasizes that the formation of the ministry had little if any impact on colonial legislation, although nominally it could be regarded as friendly to the colonies.

703. Grant, William L. *The Colonial Policy of Chatham* Kingston, 1911.

Slim pamphlet, old fashioned in approach and insensitive to both the political structures of Hanoverian Britain and the complexities of the personalities involved. Attributes to Pitt a highly progressive scheme for federal union between the American colonies and Great Britain, which if implemented, might have averted revolution and war.

704. Grant, William L. "Pitt's Theory of Empire", *Queen's Quarterly*, (July–September 1908), pp. 32–43.

Argues that Pitt's imperialism was more pragmatic—dominated by commercial considerations—than theoretical or doctrinaire. Illustrates this through a close analysis of Pitt's speech on 9 December 1762 against the Peace of Paris.

705. Greiert, Steven. "The Earl of Halifax and British Colonial Policy, 1748–1756", Duke University Ph.D. dissertation, 1976.

Chapter XII illustrates how Pitt's coming to power tended to diminish the importance of Halifax in military/colonial policy after 1756.

706. Guttridge, G. H. *English Whiggism and the American Revolution* Berkeley, 1963.

Brief but thoughtful study, valuable for relating Pitt's policy on America to the central legal, constitutional and party developments of the day. His schematization of British politics is, however, open to challenge. See: Ian Christie. *Myth and Reality in late eighteenth century British Politics* London, 1970. pp. 196–213.

707. Hall, Hubert. "Chatham's Colonial Policy", *American Historical Review*, V (July, 1900), pp. 659–675.

Examination of Pitt's colonial policy (1756–1765) and the consequences of that policy in the light of subsequent events. Credits Pitt with nearly singlehandedly winning the Seven Years War and formulating an acute, statesmanlike policy which, under better circumstances, might have averted the disastrous consequences of colonial misgovernment.

708. Harlow, Vincent. *The Founding of the Second British Empire 1763–1793* I, London, 1952. Reprinted in 1964.

A significant work, containing important sections on Pitt's views concerning colonial rights and the propriety of the Laws of Trade set within the general context of British commercial policy.

709. Hotblack, Kate. *Chatham's Colonial Policy: A Study in the Fiscal and Economic Implications of the Colonial Policy of the Elder Pitt* London, 1917. Reprinted by the Porcupine Press in 1981.

Based on original sources and still the only comprehensive analysis of Pitt's colonial policy, seen as a coherent imperial design. Includes many illustrative letters from Pitt to diplomats, admiralty, military and colonial officials.

710. Humphreys, Robert A. "Lord Shelburne and British Colonial Policy, 1766–1768", *English Historical Review*, L (April 1935), pp. 257–277.

Fundamental for the colonial policy of the Chatham ministry, but focusing on Shelburne, deals with Pitt only incidentally.

711. Johnson, Allan S. "British Politics and the Repeal of the Stamp Act", *South Atlantic Quarterly*, LXII (1963), pp. 169–186.

Important study of how Pitt's noncommittal stand on domestic political and colonial issues in the summer of 1765, adversely affected the Rockingham ministry's management of the American crisis. Politically weak at home, and lacking a statesmanlike lead, such as Pitt might have provided, the ministry failed—until too late—to develop a decisive plan of action. Johnson also demonstrates that in finally advocating repeal of the Stamp Act, Pitt was particularly influenced by the writings and arguments of the American pamphleteer, Daniel Dulany of Maryland.

712. Keller, Hans Gustav. "Pitt's Provisional Act for settling the troubles in America; das Problem der Einheit des Britischen Reichs", *Historische Zeitschrift*, CXCIV, 3 (1962), pp. 599–654.

Routine survey of the circumstances surrounding and following Chatham's proposal for conciliation with America, introduced in 1775; based on printed sources and not very illuminating.

713. Langford, Paul. *The First Rockingham Administration, 1765–1766* Oxford, 1973.

Contains important sections on the repeal of the Stamp Act, Trade Policy in 1766 and Pitt's perception of the colonial crisis.

714. Langford, Paul. "Old Whigs, Old Tories and the American Revolution", *Journal of Imperial and Commonwealth History*, (1980), pp. 106–130.

Adds Pitt's contradictory position on American taxation to his many ambiguities as statesman and politician.

715. Langford, Paul. "The Rockingham Whigs and America, 1767–1773", in *Statesmen, Scholars and Merchants: Essays in Eighteenth Century History presented to Dame Lucy Sutherland*, edited by Anne Whiteman, J. S. Bromley and P.G.M. Dickson. Oxford, 1973. pp. 135–153.

Defends the view that Pitt and the Rockingham Whigs were less supportive of the colonial cause, especially after 1767, than historians have traditionally believed.

716. Laprade, W. T. "The Stamp Act in British Politics", *American Historical Review*, XXXV (1930), pp. 735–757.

Severely critical, attributing to Pitt chief responsibility for the Chatham ministry's failure to provide political stability and to resolve the crisis in America.

717. Lawson, Philip. "George Grenville and America: The Years of Opposition, 1765–1770", *William and Mary Quarterly*, 3rd. series, 37 (1980), pp. 561–576.

Details Grenville's opposition to the American policy of the Chatham administration and emphasizes Chatham's inconsistent stand on sovereignty and taxation as a key factor in this opposition.

718. McLachlan, Jean. "The Uneasy Neutrality: A Study of Anglo-Spanish Disputes over Spanish Ships Prized, 1756–1759", *Cambridge Historical Journal*, 6 (1938–1940), pp. 55–77.

Thorough coverage of Pitt's handling of Anglo-Spanish differences over British privateers and issues in colonial trade.

719. Morgan, Edmund and Helen M. *The Stamp Act Crisis: Prologue to Revolution* Chapel Hill, 1953.

Well written narrative and analysis of Pitt's role in the repeal of the Stamp Act. Sees Pitt as a vital force in the tortuous course of British politics preceding the repeal. Could benefit from a closer investigation of British manuscript sources and a more critical reassessment of George Grenville.

720. Norris, John. *Shelburne and Reform* London, 1963.

A well written, stimulating work of research, highly critical of Pitt's erratic attitude towards America, East India and reform politics. Based on a wide range of primary source materials.

721. Perry, Keith. *British Politics and the American Revolution* New York, 1990.

A masterly digest of modern research providing a concise account of Pitt's attitude towards the Stamp Act, his conciliation proposals and his opposition to Lord North.

722. Pitman, Frank. *The Development of the British West Indies, 1700–1763* New Haven, 1917.

Provides a useful account of Pitt's efforts to check illicit commerce with the French West Indies (1755–1761). Makes the important observation that the tightening up of customs regulations in America, which made Grenville so unpopular, had already been initiated by Pitt during the Seven Years War.

723. Ritcheson, Charles. *British Politics and the American Revolution* University of Oklahoma Press, Norman, 1954.

Exhaustive study, particularly important for the attention given to the factors shaping Pitt's concept of "federalized" Empire, novel in the author's view, and for illustrating the negative impact of party divisions on attempts to resolve the American problem.

724. Ritcheson, Charles. "The Elder Pitt and an American department", *American Historical Review*, LVII, nr. 2 (1952), pp. 376–383.

Examines Pitt's idea of creating a separate department for American affairs and the reasons for the abandonment of that proposal.

725. Robbins, Caroline. *The Eighteenth Century Commonwealth* New York, 1968.

Denies that Pitt ever had any constructive ideas on colonial relations or a true desire—and aptitude—for fundamental political reform.

726. Sainsbury, John. *Disaffected Patriots: London Supporters of Revolutionary America, 1769–1782* Kingston/Montreal, 1987.

Shows how the waning of Pitt's influence among metropolitan opposition by 1770 weakened the effectiveness and prestige of the extra-parliamentary, pro-American movement based in London.

727. Sainsbury, John. "The Pro-Americans of London, 1769–1782", *William and Mary Quarterly*, 35 (1978), pp. 423–454.

Makes the important point that the Chatham administration's pro-American sympathies were more limited in scope and pragmatic in intention than traditionally believed.

728. Siebenick, Henry. "William Pitt, Earl of Chatham and the taxation of America", *Western Pennsylvania Historical Magazine*, XXVI, (1943), pp. 1–20.

Attributes Pitt's finespun separation of the power to tax from legislative sovereignty to a coherent imperial philosophy but signally fails to describe or interpret that philosophy. Also does not appreciate the problematic nature of Pitt's speeches as reported by the contemporary press.

729. Sosin, Jack. *Agents and Merchants: British Colonial Policy and the Origins of the American Revolution, 1763–1775* Lincoln, 1965.

Suggests that the Chatham ministry's inability to lessen Anglo-American tensions, despite initial hopes, was due to internal political weakness, the unresolved problem of financing North American defense, coupled with renewed American challenges to the British Mutiny Act and imperial trade legislation. British counter measures, designed to buttress Parliamentary authority, subsequently provoked the colonists to still further resistance, thereby creating a process of escalation leading to the final crisis.

730. Spector, Margaret. *The American Department of British Government, 1768–1782* New York, 1940. Reprinted by Octagon Books in 1976.

Of interest for its discussion of Pitt's position on the creation of a separate Colonial Department.

731. Temperley, Harold. "Chatham, North and America", *Quarterly Review*, 221 (October, 1914), pp. 295–319.

Outdated in its conception of 18th. century British politics, but presents an interesting analysis of Chatham's ideas for redesigning the administrative and economic structure of imperial government after the Seven Years War. Concludes that Chatham's economic policy in particular, emphasizing more effective British control of trade, could never have settled the commercial disputes at issue or secured essential colonial assent, despite his otherwise imaginative sympathy for American ideals.

732. Thomas, P.D.G. *British Politics and the Stamp Act Crisis* Oxford, 1975.

A fine, intelligently argued work, essential for the policies of the Chatham administration as they related to the American problem. Views policy as the product of the complicated interaction between King, Parliament, Cabinet, public opinion and colonial agents.

733. Thomas, P.D.G. "Charles Townshend and American Taxation in 1767", *English Historical Review*, (1968), pp. 33–51.

Illustrates how Chatham's illness in 1767 gave Townshend the opportunity to influence governmental and colonial policy. He is critical of the Chatham party's weak resistance to Townshend's revenue proposals and questions their claim to be considered "friends of America".

734. Toohey, Robert. *Liberty and Empire: British Radical Solutions to the American Problem 1774–1776* Lexington, 1978.

Offers valuable insights into Chatham's views on America and his attitude towards British radical thinking on the American crisis.

735. Tucker, Robert and Hendrickson, David. *The Fall of the First British Empire: Origins of the War of American Independence* Baltimore, 1982.

The authors focus due attention on the inconsistencies between Chatham's condemnation of colonial actions while in office and his pleas for toleration and conciliation once he was in opposition. They also note that Chatham's plan for conciliation presented in 1775 clearly failed to address the defects and uncertainties that had characterized the past operation of the Anglo-Colonial system. The book concludes that faced with an inescapable option—the certain loss of the colonies without war or the remote hope of retaining the colonies by employing force—it is almost certain that had Chatham been in power after 1770, he would have been drawn into conflict in the same fashion as the North ministry had been drawn.

736. Van Alstyne, Richard. "Europe, the Rockingham Whigs and the War for American Independence: Some Documents", *Huntington Library Quarterly*, XXV (1961), pp. 1–28.

Provides important perspectives on Chatham's colonial policy on the basis of letters from the Rockingham manuscripts. Also uses the American issue to explain why there was no political union between Chatham and the Rockingham opposition parties.

737. Williams, Basil. "Chatham and the Representation of the Colonies in the Imperial Parliament", *English Historical Review*, 22 (October 1907), pp. 756–758.

Prints Chatham's two plans of 1770 for the inclusion of Irish and American colonial representatives. Includes an introduction and notes.

XIII.   Portraits, Cartoons and Statues, etc.

738. Pitt was a favourite subject of graphic satire and most of the political prints in which he featured have been meticulously listed and described in: F. G. Stephens and D. George eds. *Catalogue of Political and Personal Satires Preserved in the Department of Prints and Drawings in the British Museum* volumes 6–8, London, 1938–1947. (reprinted 1978) Many of the important prints, drawn from various sources are also reproduced in: Herbert Atherton. *Political Prints in the Age of Hogarth* Oxford, 1974, pp. 251–258 and in the appendix.

See also: John Brewer ed. *The Common People and Politics 1750–1790* Cambridge, 1986; H. T. Dickinson ed. *Caricatures and the Constitution 1760–1832* Cambridge, 1986; D. George. *English Political Caricature to 1792* Oxford, 1959 (plates 35, 37, 39, 41, 46, 47b).

All the prints in the British Library are available in microfilm published by Chadwyck-Healey Ltd., Cambridge, 1978.

739. Carretta, Vincent. *George III and the Satirists from Hogarth to Byron* London, 1990.

Reproduces and analyzes the more important prints relating to Pitt. A valuable supplement to Atherton.

740. The most famous portrait of Chatham is that produced by Richard Brompton. The original was presented by Chatham to Philip, second Earl of Stanhope in 1772 and is now at Chevening. It was engraved in line by J. K. Sherwin in 1784 and in mezzotint by E. Fisher. There is a replica in the National Portrait Gallery, London and in the New York Public Library.

741. Hart, Charles. "Peale's allegory of William Pitt, Earl of Chatham", *Massachusetts Historical Society Proceedings*, XLVIII (1915), pp. 291–303.

Provides a brief history, with illustrative letters, of Charles Willson Peale's mezzotint allegory of Pitt, completed in 1770–1771.

742. Sellers, C. "Virginia's great allegory of William Pitt", *William and Mary Quarterly*, 3rd. series, IX (1952), pp. 58–66.

Discusses Charles Willson Peale's allegorical portrait. Shows that although little more than an inflated political cartoon, Peale's work, commissioned in 1767 by the gentry of Westmoreland county, was warmly received in Virginia.

743. The most notable statues of Pitt are those created by Joseph Wilton and John Bacon. One of Wilton's statues was commissioned by the City of Cork and completed in 1766, another by the City of New York in 1768 and a third was contracted by the Assembly of North Carolina and erected in Charleston in 1770. John Bacon's monument to Chatham is in Westminster Abbey and dates from 1779.

744. Smith, D. E. "Wilton's Statute of Pitt", *South Carolina Historical Magazine*, XV (1914), pp. 18–38.

Outlines the events, with supporting documentation, leading to the decision by the State of South Carolina to commission a statue in honour of Pitt, following the repeal of the Stamp Act in 1766.

745. Wali, A. J. "The Statues of King George III and the Honourable William Pitt erected in New York City 1770", *New York Historical Society, Quarterly Bulletin*, 4 (1920), pp. 37–57.

Traces the history of these statues, both commissioned simultaneously, executed by the same sculptor in London, both erected in New York the same year (1770) and both destroyed six years later, the remains stored in the New York room of the New York Historical Society.

746. Whinney, Margaret. *Sculpture in Britain, 1530–1830* London, 1964.

Provides plate (129b) and short history of John Bacon's monument to Chatham in Westminster Abbey, completed in 1779.

XIV.   Places Associated with William Pitt, Earl of Chatham

747. Cork Street, Burlington Gardens, London.

From 1741 until his appointment as Paymaster in 1746, Pitt had rooms in Cork Street, though he usually spent the summer and autumn visiting various friends in the country.

748. South Lodge, Enfield Chace

Pitt bought this house, on 65 acres, from Lady Charlotte Edwin in 1747 and sold it in 1753. In the Chatham MSS 74 are three rough sketches, evidently by Pitt, of various landscape designs.

749. The Circus, Bath.

Dependent upon the waters at Bath, Pitt in 1754 built a house at number 7, The Circus, Bath, a fashionable part of the city where Clive and Gainsborough also had houses. He sold the dwelling in 1763, the year of his breach with the Corporation of Bath.

750. Chatham House, 9/10 St. James Square, London, WC1.

Pitt lived there from 1756 to 1761 while Secretary of State. It is now the location of the Royal Institute of International Affairs.

751. Hayes Place, Kent.

Pitt's country house, purchased in 1756 and sold to Thomas Walpole in 1766. Pitt then repurchased it in 1767. The house has since been demolished. Chatham Avenue, Bromley, roughly corresponds to the original location of the house and garden.

752. Burton Pynsent, near Langport, Somerset.

This was an estate inherited by Pitt from Sir William Pynsent in 1765. This was Pitt's main residence where he engaged in substantial and expensive alterations that contributed so heavily to the financial plight of later years. Today the only part of Burton Pynsent left intact is the west wing, the main building having been demolished in 1805.

753. North End House, Hampstead.

The house of one Charles Dingley, where Pitt spent some months in 1766–1767 recovering from physical and mental collapse.

754. Collinson, John. *History and Antiquities of Somerset* 3 vols. Bath, 1791.

Includes an account and illustrations of Pitt's estate Burton Pynsent.

755. Barratt, T. J. *Annals of Hampstead* London, 1910.

Contains a drawing of Chatham's room in North End House by A. B. Quinton.

756. Lysons, D. *Environs of London* 5 vols. London, 1792–1811.

Contains information about South Lodge and Enfield Chace.

757. Thorne, J. *Environs of London* London, 1876.

Contains a good discussion of Pitt's construction at Enfield Chace and Hayes.

758. [Whateley, Thomas]. *Observations on Modern Gardening* London, 1801.

Includes information about Pitt's South Lodge.

Index to Authors

The numbers cited are entry numbers.

Index to Correspondents and Subjects

The numbers cited are entry numbers.

ABOUT THE AUTHOR

KARL W. SCHWEIZER is Professor of History at the New Jersey Institute of Technology. He is the author of many books and articles, including most recently, *England, Prussia, and the Seven Years War* (1989) and *Cobbett in His Times* (1990). Dr. Schweizer is also a Fellow of the British Royal Historical Society.

www.ingramcontent.com/pod-product-compliance
Lightning Source LLC
Chambersburg PA
CBHW070443100426
42812CB00004B/1194